Rejoice

Philippians 4:4

the thirty-five year mission journey of Ray and Joyce Rogers

I Thess. 5: 16-18
Thank you for your faithful
service for our Lord!
May this book bring
you a special blessing.

Joyce Campbell Rogers

Joyce C. Rogers

Rejoice

Joyce Campbell Rogers

PUBLISHED BY:
BRENTWOOD CHRISTIAN PRESS
WWW.BRENTWOODBOOKS.COM
1-800-334-8861

Dedication

This book is dedicated to a number of special people:

To my husband, Ray, who has shared these experiences with me. A fifty year journey of serving and working together as servants of our Lord has been a rich blessing. I could not have written this book without his encouragement, his helpful advice, his loving kindness, and his gentle spirit.

To Christopher John, our son, who experienced a great part of the journey with us. For his sacrifice of separation from loved ones, and for his support for our calling and ministry, we salute him and thank him.

To our daughter-in-law, Anna, who experienced her own journey as a missionary kid.

To our two grandsons, Christopher Ray, and William Lewis, that "they would put their trust in God, and would not forget His deeds but would keep His commands." (Psalm 78:7)

To my brothers, Reese and John Campbell, and my sister-in-law, Ernestine Rogers Rochelle, for their prayer support throughout the years.

And to Southern Baptists who prayed and supported us through the Cooperative Program and the Lottie Moon Christmas Offerings.

Acknowledgements

I give praise and gratitude to God for providing the right person to come along beside me at a crucial time to guide me in the writing process. I am indebted to Carol Hill (Mrs. Stephen) for her invaluable advice, words of encouragement, and for the many hours she spent reading and editing the manuscript. I am grateful for her unusual ability to correct without discouraging, and to guide without dominating.

Thanks to Linda Gilden for her candid advice and suggestions, and for reading parts of the manuscript.

Thanks also to my friend, Mary Gregg (Mrs. John) for doing the final copy edit of the manuscript.

And lastly I am indebted to my mother and to my sister, Helen, (both of whom are with the Lord) for saving many of our letters through the years, some dating back to the early sixties.

Foreword

The Lord has consistently worked throughout the life of Joyce Rogers in the context of His love for a lost world. As a college student, she heard a missionary speak, tears flowed, and the impact of a world without Christ lingered in her heart. As a young married woman, she was asked, "Young lady, have you considered that God may want you to take His gospel overseas?" The poignant question was engraved on her heart. God must have smiled that evening in 1960 when Joyce and husband Ray responded to the call to go wherever He would lead. Little did they know that His plan for them would include 35 years of overseas ministry with numerous people groups in at least seven countries!

My husband, Jerry, and I had the joy of working alongside the Rogers in Indonesia and often sought their wise counsel and prayer support. Their passion to proclaim the gospel among Muslim villagers in East Java was undeterred by the lack of roads, the debilitating tropical climate, and religious opposition. Numerous churches were planted, new believers discipled, and indigenous leaders trained in ministry. Ray and Joyce were models to missionary colleagues in their faithfulness and perseverance in prayer. Their walk with the Lord was unquestionably authentic.

The theme of the Rogers' pilgrimage could appropriately be, "We have seen the Lord." An aborted communist coup d'etat in Indonesia was followed by winds of revival that launched their fruitful ministry. Grief in having to leave their beloved country after twenty-six years was transformed to joy as they saw God greatly expand ministry opportunities throughout South and Southeast Asia.

You will be amazed at the greatness of God as you take the journey with Ray and Joyce to the Khond Hills of Orissa in India, enter the longhouses of Sarawak in Malaysia, visit the Karen refugees on the Thai-Burma border, and read about people long held in the bondage of darkness, now set free to serve the one true God! This book will give you a fresh vision of God's glory and His power in the world today. Prepare to gain a clearer vision of missions as you are challenged by the testimony of two of God's choicest servants. As you read *Rejoice*, you, too, may be confronted with that question once posed to Joyce, "Have you considered that God may want you to take His gospel overseas?"

Bobbye Rankin, former Missionary to Indonesia and wife of Jerry Rankin, President of International Mission Board, SBC

Table of Contents

❧

Part 1
God Calls

❧

Introduction

A new fallen, early morning snow brightened my arrival into this world on January 2, 1936. I was child number five for S. Mortimer and Bessie Garrison Campbell. I joined Reese, Marion, Helen and John in a home where Christ was magnified. They named me Alice Joyce, Alice for my maternal grandmother.

My parents were farmers. With strong faith and hard work, they purchased the Bethea farm in 1932. The farm was located in Claussen, ten miles from Florence, South Carolina. Our antebellum home sat back from the main road, picturesquely nestled among large pecan trees. This place stayed in our family close to seventy years.

When I came along in 1936, there was no indoor plumbing, no phone service, and no electricity. For lighting, we used kerosene lamps that were cleaned everyday. We all worked hard on the farm and in the home. Even though we were not wealthy with money, we had more than enough food of all kinds that was grown and raised on the farm. My parents were well respected and were often sought out for advice and counsel in the community. Relatives, friends, and neighbors all enjoyed coming to our home. My mom, without doubt, was one of the world's best cooks.

The church was a central part of our lives. We were members of the Willow Creek Baptist Church in the Florence Association. This church and Mizpah Baptist were established by my maternal great grandfather, Rev. Robert Napier. Dad served over sixty years as a deacon at Willow Creek. I learned early that prayer was important. I recall praying about everything, from the closest neighbor, to the faraway people in China. Even our enemy, Hitler, was brought to our Father in prayer. I recall that my dad never prayed a prayer without including, "Apart from you we can do nothing, but with you all things are possible."

Several of my early childhood prayers were answered, and this encouraged me to pray even more. I remember a particular prayer meeting when a small group of adults were praying at my home church, Willow Creek Baptist. I was the only child in the group that evening. My dad explained that we needed a communion set. The one our church owned was old and needed to be replaced. He encouraged the group to pray that the Lord would open the way for funds to be provided. The very next morning, my uncle, who was a member of a nearby Baptist Church, called to say that they had a new communion set and wanted to offer their old one to our church. He mentioned that the previous night, while at prayer meeting, the Lord put the idea in their minds. This was a deciding moment for me as a child that prayer was important, and that God did hear and answer prayers.

As far back as I can remember, I have always loved the Lord. When I was twelve years old, I made a public decision to accept Christ as Savior and Lord. For several years, I had believed but had not made my decision public.

On a weekly basis we listened to Billy Graham's broadcast. I caught from his messages the urgency of sharing the gospel. He always told those that made decisions that their family and friends would wait for them if they came forward to accept Christ. As a young child, while looking for violets and wildflowers in the woods nearby our home, I would enjoy pretending to preach the gospel. The trees served as my audience as I brought the message and invited my "congregation" in my best Billy Graham voice to "Come, Come, just as you are! Your friends and family will wait on you!" Those trees had hard hearts like some people. I could never get them to come forward!

We did not have regular worship services at our church during this period in my life. We shared a pastor with another sister church, and we would have worship only twice a month. I was baptized in a river nearby to our church, which had the same name as our church. My baptism took place in November, and it was very cold. I was baptized along with two adults.

My mom led the way to establish our first mission organization. She talked with the ladies about organizing the Woman's Missionary Society (WMS), which would be equivalent today to our Women on Mission organization. Since we did not have any youth mission organizations, I went with her to the meetings. Mom ordered the *Royal Service* magazine, and each woman paid for her own subscription. When the magazine arrived each month, I read it from cover to cover. The ladies gave me the responsibility of presenting the prayer calendar, sharing the names of the missionaries who had birthdays. I learned about the missionaries serving in places with strange sounding names. Little did I know that one day my own name would be on the prayer calendar.

At the age of fifteen, I surrendered to full time Christian service. This took place at Ridgecrest Baptist Assembly. Dr. C. Roy Angel was the speaker that week, and he shared the importance of giving one's life to the Lord.

Shortly after that, I entered the Better Speakers Tournament sponsored by the Baptist Training Union. The title of my speech was, "Jesus is the Way." I was declared runner-up in our Florence Association. I was beginning to see that God could use me!

A few years later I entered once again. This time I won the associational and regional contests, and came in second in the state contest. The Lord was developing and strengthening me for His service.

While a student at North Greenville Jr. College (now North Greenville University), I had many opportunities to hear missionaries speak on campus. Each time, I was deeply moved by their messages, even to tears. I often thought about what they had shared long after they had left the campus. I talked with some close friends about their reaction to the messages. While they were moved with compassion, the messages seemingly did not linger with them. I came to the conclusion that God was dealing with me in some certain way, even though I did not understand what it meant.

Upon graduation from college, I became the first, full-time, support-staff person at Calvary Baptist in Florence. I was hired as the administrative assistant and secretary to the pastor. That simply meant I did everything!

Dr. Elbert H. Walker and wife, Dorothy (Dottie), had been at Calvary for about three years when I joined them. They had two children, Scott and Donna. Dr. Walker shared with me about two months after I started working at the church that he and Dottie had answered the call to foreign missions. This was information he was not yet ready to share with the church, and he requested that I not share this news with anyone.

The following months, I walked through the entire appointment process with them, from preparing their life histories, to filling out doctrinal question forms. I know now that the Lord was preparing me at the same time that he was leading the Walkers to answer their call. God was getting several servants ready all at the same time, but I was completely unaware of how He was working.

Ray Rogers came into my life when he was hired as an associate to Dr. Walker for the summer months of 1955. Ray was over six feet tall, and had black hair, brown eyes, and a huge smile. The first thing I noticed was the joy he exuded. His main job was to work with Vacation Bible School and the youth. During this time, he had a fifteen minute radio program, "Hymns for all Churches," five days a week. His parents, Jesse Clifton Rogers and Flossie were members at Calvary. His dad worked as a machinist on the railroad. Of the two girls and four boys in the family, Ray was the youngest. Ray had just graduated from Wake Forest University. I found him to be very outgoing and a very happy individual. I learned quickly that he was a gifted speaker and a very talented singer. As the days and weeks of working together went by, we became friends.

After Dr Walker and his family were appointed as missionaries to the Philippines, they left Calvary in 1957. They were assigned to the Seminary in Baguio, Philippines, and Calvary called Reverend J. K. Lawton. He had a heart for missions, as his sister was a missionary. I had the pleasure of working with him for almost a year before Ray and I were married.

During the time that Ray and I were going together, he was attending Southeastern Baptist Theological Seminary, and we often talked about missions. I recall on one occasion Ray had been deeply touched by a message that one of his Seminary professors had brought to the students. The professor had made the statement, "Never rule in a state pastorate until you can rule out a foreign call." This statement had a great impact on him. We both wanted to do God's will and often prayed about missions, but I don't think either of us knew that we would be called!

Upon Ray's graduation from seminary in May, 1958, we were married the following month. Together, we served the First Baptist Church in Turbeville, SC. It was a small community with a wonderful fellowship of Christ-loving individuals. Ray had the opportunity to lead these dear people in a building program, and we helped organize all the mission organizations.

On one occasion, a lady missionary from the nearby Methodist church spoke, and we were invited to hear her. She came up to me before the service and spoke to me directly. She said, "Young lady, have you considered that God may want you to take His gospel overseas?" I had not even been introduced to her. Her statement lingered in my heart and mind.

We were given the opportunity to attend the Southern Baptist Convention in Miami in 1960. While there, we attended Dr. C. Roy Angel's church, Central Baptist, and heard Dr. Baker James Cauthen. Dr. Cauthen was the executive secretary of the Foreign Mission Board at that time. It was in that service the Lord made clear that he meant business.

Dr. Cauthen said with great passion, "There are men and women in rice paddy fields up to their knees in mud out there in Southeast Asia that know nothing about a God above who loves them and died for them. Will YOU go and tell them?"

We left the building and went to our car. Ray got in on the driver's side, leaned over the steering wheel, and put his head down. Speaking softly, he shared that God had called him that evening.

It was almost more than my heart could take! The overwhelming joy to learn that He had called us together that evening! I could barely speak over my emotions but managed to respond, "He called me, also!"

Once we were back in our hotel room, we got down on our knees beside the bed and prayed, "Lord, if you want us to go as your servants to share your love and message of salvation with people who haven't heard, then continue to lay this burden on us. But, if you would prefer that we remain in the states and serve you faithfully here, then please make it clear to us!"

A few months later we were called to another church located near Walterboro, SC. As we continued to search out God's will for the future, faithfulness to this work which God had given us in the present prepared us for the mission field. We were able to overcome many obstacles, and we learned how to be flexible and patient.

We spent two and a half years in this pastorate when we were called to a much larger church near Camden, SC. If we answered the call to the church, we would have to stay at least two years before we could be eligible for appointment for mission service. We knew that it was time to settle the question of whether or not we would answer His call to missions or continue on in the pastorate. We wrote two letters, one accepting and one rejecting the offer to the church. We went in separate rooms of our home and prayed for a long period of time. When we came together, it was obvious that we needed to make a decision for missions.

We made plans to attend Foreign Mission Week at Ridgecrest that summer. It was very important to us that we make a decision, not based on emotional compassion, but based upon the full knowledge and awareness that the Lord was calling us to go.

That Sunday morning after Dr. Cauthen preached, we made a public declaration that we were presenting ourselves for career, mission service. We both were convinced that we were called, and we never doubted that call throughout the thirty-five years we served.

When the mission representative spoke with us, he inquired as to what part of the world we might be considering.

We both answered, "The Orient," without having discussed where we might serve. Southeast Asia was referred to as the "Orient" in those days.

Our decision was really based on the fact that more people lived in the Orient who had not had the opportunity to hear the good news of Jesus Christ. We met with Dr. Winston Crawley, Secretary to the Orient, and he suggested places we could serve.

Our appointment as career missionaries to Indonesia was on April 9, 1963. We spent fourteen days in orientation at Mars Hill College, in July of 1963, and departed for the field in August.

Preparing for Departure

"By faith Abraham, when called to go to a place he would
later receive as his inheritance, obeyed and went,
even though he did not know where he was going."
Hebrews 11:8

Returning from our appointment service of April 9, 1963, in Richmond, Virginia, I became nauseated on-board the plane. After arriving back home, I continued to have bouts of nausea and dizziness. I felt tired and sluggish. Ray encouraged me to call my doctor to determine the problem. It was *not* a good time to feel under the weather with all the preparation that lay ahead for us.

The doctor ran some tests and said that he would call me with the results. Two days later, he called to share some long awaited, good news. I could hear the excitement in the doctor's voice, "Mrs. Rogers, you are pregnant!"

A look of sheer joy was on Ray's face when he heard the good news. We had been married for five years and had been in prayer for a child for over three years by this time. We paused and thanked God for answering our prayers. We added to our prayer of thanksgiving a prayer of concern for a safe and healthy pregnancy.

Our Father's timing is always perfect. We not only could prepare for our baby's needs for the future days, but the greatest blessing the Lord gave was the fact that our child was with us when we were called forward for mission work at our appointment service. We knew we were blessed together *as a family* to carry His Word to the lost.

During our Orientation, which took place in July 1963 at Mars Hill College, we met two couples who were scheduled to depart along with us from Los Angeles. The Foreign Mission Board had booked passage for us on a passenger liner leaving out of Los Angeles, but when the personnel on the ship found out that I was expecting, they refused to allow me to travel with them. Ray and I were disappointed that we would travel by plane, without having the companionship of the other two missionary couples. Several months later, we heard that a gambling party was on board from Los Angeles to Honolulu, and they needed our cabin. Also, the stormy weather on the sea caused the passengers to get seasick. What seemed like a disappointment at first, actually turned out to be a blessing instead. Most likely I was spared getting sick!

We had three weeks after our Orientation at Mars Hill to prepare to leave. Those final weeks were like a whirlwind of activities: shopping, sorting, packing, and crating larger items. We had to think about living in a country where all electrical appliances ran on 50 cycles. We placed a special order for a 50 cycle refrigerator, a wringer washing machine, a pasteurizer, and other items that would be useful for our new lifestyle. We were anxious that they arrive on time to be crated.

News had come from Singapore that we could purchase a kerosene stove there that produced a gas flame, using an instrument inside called a gasifier. This was a cleaner process than the regular kerosene stove which produced a lot of black soot.

We managed to get it all done and had a few quiet days to be with our family before the departure day arrived. It was a beautiful, hot August day in 1963. Many family and friends were at the airport to see us off. This was our first among many departures over the years. It was always a bitter-sweet experience that never became easy.

A myriad of thoughts and emotions were swirling through my mind and heart that morning. We were embarking on a journey unknown. As Ray and I stood together and prayed for His strength, His guidance, and His protection over each step along the way, we took comfort in the certainty of His call and His promise that He would never forsake us.

I rode to the airport with my mom and dad. Ray rode with his parents that morning. I recall that my mom and dad were very quiet. I know that many things were probably flashing through their minds that morning, but very little was said as we rode to the airport. Our hearts were full, and my parents seemed to savor our being together in quietness. I have often thought about what they were likely feeling and thinking that day.

I was their youngest child. I was six months pregnant. I was going to the other side of the world. The times were different then. It would take three weeks to a month for an air-o-gram to reach us. Telephone calls were expensive and not clear if we got through to our party. There was no clicking of the mouse to send an instant message. It was before the days of the Blackberry, video cameras, etc. It would be five years before they would see me again. The child I was carrying wouldn't know them for a long time. There would be many family events that *we* would miss. I knew that they had already mentioned the possibility that one or both of them may not be alive when we returned. To return home in the event of the death of a parent in those days was rare. Still, they wanted us to know that they gave their full support and blessing to our mission service. They also were willing to make sacrifices for us to answer God's call. Ray's parents felt that way as well. Riding in the backseat of the car, I prayed a silent prayer for them, "Lord, may your grace to be sufficient for us at this moment."

Ray's dad was one in the group that day who would not be present when we returned home five years later. He went to be with the Lord the year before we were due furlough.

When they called for us to board the plane, Ray got up from his seat, hugged his parents, said, "I'll see you all in five years," and turning away, waved good-bye. He was waiting for me at the top of the steps while I went to each individual to say my good-byes. After all these years of saying good-bye at airports, I believe his is the best method.

Departure to the field

The itinerary that the Board booked for us was departure out of Florence, SC, to Atlanta, GA, and on to San Francisco. We spent the night in San Francisco, having arrived there in the evening.

Reservations were made for us to stay in a hotel on the waterfront downtown. It was a breezy day and very cool. Throughout the city, there were arrays of colorful flowers. Breakfast the next morning included rhubarb with thick cream, which was a first for us. It has been a favorite of mine since that time.

We shipped a large footlocker by air freight. Ray found the place in the terminal where this could be done. It was late at night. Only one person was on duty, and he appeared to be inebriated. His face was flushed red and he was beginning to slur his words.

I said to Ray, "We must try to find someone else to help us." In the meantime, he presented a form for us to sign. Ray requested a copy of the form.

He leaned over the counter and snapped, "I'll take care of it!" He appeared agitated with us that we were questioning him. He kept slurring out, "It is not necessary!"

We hung around for a couple of minutes, thinking we could wait for some positive results, but it was fruitless. Ray walked away praying, "Lord, please protect our needed supplies in the footlocker and send it to us safely."

I had doubts that we would see it again!

The second day of our journey we left California and flew to Hawaii on British Airlines. We were to stay overnight in Honolulu and were scheduled to depart on the same plane the next afternoon.

I had flown only one other time in my life; Ray had traveled by air short distances on several occasions. It was a first for each of us in many ways, not having traveled overseas. We were from the rural, segregated south, and now we were on a plane with mixed-race couples and people from other countries. Japanese stewardesses were on board, working right alongside the British crew. It was a perfect introduction to the diversity of people in the world, all of whom God loves.

Friends had sent word to Rev. Jim Harley, a former pastor of the Evergreen Baptist Church in the Florence association, and to Ray's niece, Barbara Goodwin Shepherd, that we would be stopping in Honolulu. Jim was working with the Baptist Convention, and Barbara and her husband were stationed there in the military. We didn't know if they would be at the airport or not, but we were straining to look for them once we arrived.

We rejoiced when we saw them! It was good to see familiar faces. They both brought flower leis to place around our necks to welcome us Hawaiian style.

British Airlines put us in the hotel Moana, located right on the beach. A famous Hawaiian radio program called, "Hawaiian Calls" broadcast from the hotel each evening from under a huge, old, Banyan tree in the yard of the hotel on the seaside. The sounds of the ocean waves breaking, the cool island breeze blowing gently, the sounds of soothing music were all comforting and relaxing to us after an exciting but long day.

Our journey continued the next afternoon to Tokyo. The same crew was on board, including the captain. It was at least an hour into the flight when the captain spoke to us from the flight deck. He said that he would be coming through the cabin to greet us shortly. A well-built, tall gentleman sporting a trimmed, white beard appeared in the cabin. His hair was like a cloud of silver grey. He spoke with a heavy British accent and shook hands with every passenger. He paused when he got to us. He inquired as to our destination, etc. We shared with him the purpose of our journey. He seemed intrigued. As he was moving away, he looked back and said, "Blessings on you!" In all of our travels, we never had another captain to come through and speak to the passengers as this captain did.

Arrival in Tokyo was late evening. My heart skipped a beat with joy when I saw the sign, "Ray and Joyce Rogers." Holding that sign was George Hays, treasurer of the Baptist Mission in Tokyo. He greeted us and took us to a hotel. The ceiling of the hotel was about six feet in height. Ray had to walk with his head bowed as we made our way to the room. The physical environment created a sense of being pressed down.

The next morning was Sunday, and George said that he would come to get us for church. This gave us an opportunity to meet several Southern Baptist missionaries assigned there. On the way to church, it started to rain. The sky was cloudy grey. We both felt weary. Jet lag was setting in big time. We could easily feel homesick among so many people with whom we could not communicate. We could not understand their language, and they could not understand ours. This was uncharted territory, observing and experiencing a culture that was such a contrast to ours.

We found comfort as we prayed aloud and read some scripture verses that we had written down. Ray had them in his pocket so we would have easy access to them.

I Thess.5:24 "The one who calls you is faithful and he will do it."

Jeremiah 29:11 " 'For I know the plans I have for you,' declares the Lord, 'plans to prosper you and not to harm you, plans to give you hope and a future.' "

Matt. 28:19-20 "Therefore go and make disciples of all nations, baptizing them in the name of the Father and of the Son and of the Holy Spirit, and teaching them to obey everything I have commanded you. And surely I am with you always to the very end of the age."

These were a few among many that we read. And it helped. God's word never fails to comfort when needed.

The next day, we flew to Hong Kong. Once again we were greeted by caring missionaries – Logan Templeton and Charles Cowherd. They were perfect hosts, taking us to see the city, introducing us to the shopping, and to Chinese food. We were there three days. Landing and taking off required great skill on the part of the pilots in Hong Kong, as the runway extended out to the water. We were grateful that we had no problems arriving or departing under those circumstances.

As our journey took us closer to our territory, we began to feel the excitement of getting to our place of assignment. We both had remained well on the trip, but we were looking forward to our final arrival.

Sid and Alwilda Reber and Lily Rogers were holding a sign with our names on it at the Singapore airport. They took us to the Orchid Road Hotel where we met another couple assigned to Malaysia. The Singapore missionaries were very thoughtful and kind to us. We were their guests for five days. It was a blessing to be in their homes for food and fellowship. They made sure that we got the opportunity to purchase our Phillips kerosene stove that burned a blue flame for cooking. That stove served us well for many years.

We felt loved and rested as we looked forward to the place we would call "home" for several months while waiting for our visa to Indonesia.

❧

Part 2

First Term

❧

Islands and Cities of Indonesia

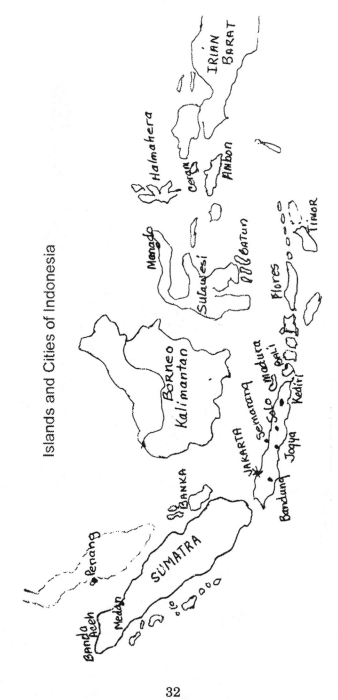

Penang... Our First Assignment

"Trust in the LORD with all your heart and lean not on your own understanding." Proverbs 3:5

On the way to Penang, our plane landed in Kuala Lumpur to refuel and to let off and pick up passengers. Charles "Chuck" Morris, chairman of the Malay Baptist Mission, took the time to come out to the airport to greet us, even though we did not go into the terminal. It was easy for him to pick us out as we were the only Caucasian people on board the plane. We stood outside the plane to talk. He was gracious in his welcome to us. He shared with us about his wife and two sons and some things about his work. He encouraged us with positive comments about our upcoming ministry at the Georgetown Baptist Church. He was warm and loving in his manner toward us. Several weeks later, he made a trip to Penang to visit us in our home. He spent time sharing about mission work and praying with these two novice missionaries. This began a friendship that lasted throughout the years. Chuck and his wife are now enjoying the rewards of heaven.

As we approached Penang Island, our plane landed at Butterworth, just across the channel from Penang. At that time, no airport was on the island. People went back and forth by ferry from the mainland to the island.

As we disembarked, we saw a large group waiting to greet us. At least 30 members were present from the Georgetown Baptist Church to welcome their new pastor and his wife. We were deeply touched by their enthusiastic greeting and their loving kindness that were noticeable from the outset of our stepping down on the ground

They gave me the once-over, asking, "When is the baby due?"

"Did you keep well during the trip?"

"This is your first baby so far away from home, not to worry, we will be your family."

When I heard those things, I realized I had been feeling a certain sadness that my family would not be present to share in the birth of our child. I was reminded that God never fails to provide exactly what we need, even before we ask Him. Arrival day in Penang will always be one of the highlights in my life. God's word is true that he provides mothers and fathers, brothers and sisters in His family of believers in Christ Jesus.

The lovely skyline of the island Penang, as seen from the ferry, was a beautiful sight. Along with the members of the church were Minor and Mary Davidson and Ralph Brunson, missionaries assigned to work on Penang Island. Minor and Mary Davidson were assigned to the Baptist Seminary and spoke Mandarin. Ralph and his wife, Charlotte, were assigned to the Tamil speaking Indians located there. They hold a special place in our hearts as great mentors and wonderful friends.

We were taken to Ralph and Charlotte Brunson's home, where we stayed for a few days until we could move into the house that had been rented for us. By this time, it was the end of August.

The house was located on Babington Avenue. It was owned by a tin mine outfit and was furnished. It was a rectangular-shaped house with a driveway beside the house that circled in the back around an orchid hedge. The sitting room was located at the back, and the master bedroom was up front near the street side. We called this place home for seven months before going to Indonesia.

The first thing on the agenda for me was to find a doctor and become acquainted with the hospital. They took me to a Seventh Day Adventist Hospital where I met the only American doctor assigned there. He was from Tennessee and spoke with a southern drawl that stood out among the Chinese speaking people. Between the Davidsons, the Brunsons, and the church folks, we were getting situated. Each step along the way was blessed by our wonderful Father who supplied all our needs.

We immediately inquired about the footlocker as to its arrival. No results! We thought it was lost for good. Among other important items in the footlocker were the baby clothes that we would need. Three weeks passed when one day a truck came to the house with a delivery. The man said in broken English, "Delivery... large box for you."

It was the footlocker! It took six weeks to arrive, but it arrived. We still have that footlocker!

There were many early adjustments. One was learning to drive on the left hand side of the road. Shopping was another. We were taken to a wet market to purchase fresh vegetables and fruit, fish, and chicken. We shopped in a small store called a *toko* for our sugar, flour, canned goods, etc. The sugar and flour were in large, open burlap sacks on the floor next to bags of rice. Clerks measured out everything by the kilogram, using the metric system. We needed to learn quickly what a meter, kilo, milligram meant in relationship to yards, gallons, quarts, and pints. Shopping took a long time to carry out, bargaining for good and fair prices, and going from place to place to purchase items.

The market was crowded, and everything had a designated location for the goods that were being sold. The fish were in a special section. Chickens and beef in another location. Pork had its own stall. Vegetables and fruits were somewhere else, and flowers were available as well.

We soon learned how to get to places, and we made friends among the local people. A large majority could speak some English, which was helpful to us. Otherwise, we used our hands to communicate.

Georgetown Baptist Church...
Our Assignment in Penang, Malaysia

The Georgetown Baptist Church got its name from the city of Georgetown on Penang Island, which was named for King George. The British occupied Penang for a period of time. Lord Cornwallis was even stationed in Penang for several years; he traveled around the world during his military years.

There were many professional people in the church. The Oh family members were pillars of the church. There were several brothers in the Oh family, and two of them were medical doctors. Also, there were several lawyers, professors, teachers, nurses, and most of them spoke several languages. The church members came from various backgrounds and ethnic groups, mainly Chinese speaking and a few Indians who spoke Tamil. English was the main language used in the church. Most of the people in the congregation came out of Buddhism and Hinduism to Christianity.

We were grateful we did not have to learn a language while in Penang as we would have to learn the Indonesian language once we arrived there. We did pick up words in Mandarin and Tamil to greet folks.

It was our first time to experience secret believers. A young, Indian, female professor was a believer and desired to come to prayer meeting on Wednesdays. Her folks embraced the Hindu religion. She could leave her home on Wednesday afternoon as she had an excuse to attend a meeting at the University that afternoon. She had a special path to the church. She would drive her car to a nearby restaurant

37

and walk from the yard of the restaurant to a side street to reach the church. She continued to be faithful in attendance while we were there.

A young man living next door to the church listened to the morning sermon from the window of his house, which was close to the church sanctuary. He found Christ as his savior by listening to the sermon from the yard and window of his house. One day, he rode his bicycle to our home to tell us that he was a believer. His parents were Buddhist and would not allow him to attend church. We prayed with him and gave him some materials to study. We extended him an open invitation to visit us at anytime. He thanked us graciously. We never did see him again.

Many opportunities were presented to bring people into the Kingdom of God. One man who stands out came on his own to the Georgetown Baptist Church. He had been seeking peace for many years in various places and ways. Nothing brought the peace that he was seeking.

One Sunday morning he showed up at the church. He came in and sat on the back row where I was seated. It was evident he was interested in everything that was happening in the service that day. He sat on the edge of his seat as he listened intently to Ray's message telling about Jesus and His love for the lost. Before Ray ended the message, he explained very clearly how to accept Christ as Savior. When we all stood to sing the invitation hymn, George Tham Sik Chew practically ran forward. This is what he shared:

For many years I sought peace with God by going to many different places such as temples, mosque, quiet parks, religious landmarks, and to churches. This morning I heard for the first time about the One that I have been seeking. I finally know His name! I have felt the peace of Jesus Christ flood over me this morning.

The best way for me to describe what has happened would be a beautifully decorated cake. The cake looks so beautiful to the eye, but you'll not ever know how wonderful it really is until you taste of it. This morning I have tasted, and I know it is good!

The next Sunday, George arrived at church with five of his colleagues from the office of the Clerk of Court where he worked. George's car was a little small, box-like car, and to see six people climb out was a sight. He shared that his aim and goal was for all from his office to know Christ as Lord and Savior.

This precious new Christian grew quickly in the Lord. He became a faithful Sunday School teacher, deacon, Sunday School Director, and a ministry leader during his years in the church. He won most everyone in his office to Christ ... including a judge.

George spent his lunch hour sitting on a bench in the yard of the courthouse praying for a particular judge. The judge saw him from his window one day and came down to ask George why he sat all alone with his head bowed. He shared with the judge that he was praying for the salvation of his colleagues... and for the judge. The judge was so amazed George was praying for him that he asked him to share his faith. That day the judge accepted Christ as Savior, and he has continued to bear witness for Christ.

George's own wife has remained a Buddhist but often comes with him to church functions. He continues to pray for her daily.

Ray was given an opportunity to speak at the Baptist Seminary to bring the message at the chapel service. We met many of the seminary students and became acquainted with Peter Nido. Peter wanted to hear our personal testimony. He never took for granted that people were saved just because they might be serving the Lord. Peter had come from a background of Hinduism and was called to preach. He was one of the students at the seminary.

Dr. Minor Davidson was teaching his class one day in the seminary. He shared with the class the importance of witnessing for Christ. He emphasized the scripture John 14:6, "Jesus said, I am the way, the truth, and the Life, no man comes to the Father except through me."

While explaining that this was God's plan for each person to come to salvation through Jesus, Peter Nido interrupted him with a question. "Do you mean that all those people passing by this building at this very moment are lost if they do not know Jesus?"

Minor answered, "Yes, that is true!"

Peter responded. "Then why are we all sitting here! Shouldn't we all be out there?" pointing to the street outside.

After that day, he devoted his time to traveling back and forth on the ferries, speaking to as many people as would listen to him about Jesus. Peter did not think of himself, only of those who were lost. He died several years later. He spent every waking moment sharing Christ with the lost to the point that he perhaps neglected himself physically. We were in Indonesia and received a letter from Dr. Davidson telling of Peter's death. This young man blessed our lives by setting an example of one who had a great passion to win the lost. We look forward to seeing him again in heaven.

Those who accepted Christ during our ministry were baptized in the Malacca Straits off Penang Island. The mission had purchased land for a new seminary location. The seminary would be situated on a hillside that overlooked the Straits. We went out to that site for the baptism service. The road was high above the sea, and steps had been built to get down to the seaside from the main road.

One Sunday afternoon in early November, we all gathered on the beach to baptize eight people. Two of them came to the baptismal service with their suitcases. Ray made the comment, "You only need a change of clothing. Why the suitcase?" We noticed that they were uneasy.

One of the boys shared, "Our families told us that if we followed through with baptism, we could not return home. We will be considered dead."

We were at a lost as to what to say at that moment. We came from a background where everyone rejoices when one follows Christ. The next few moments on that sunny day on the beach would be etched in our minds and hearts forever. A middle age couple, Joseph and Alice Chew, took the boys by the hand and told them, "From this day you will be our children."

Years later, we learned that the families had a change of heart and took them back into their families. They had seen a positive change in the young men and knew what they had was genuine and good.

Blessed with a Son

Climbing up and down those steep steps to get to the beach for the baptismal service convinced our son, Christopher John, to come early - November 19. He showed up two to three weeks earlier than expected, according to my stateside doctor, but I think that we may have been off on our timing.

I entered the Seventh Day Adventist Hospital on Monday at twelve noon. I was prepared and placed in a holding room with about six other women, all in labor. Two were Malay women, and three were Chinese. I was the only Caucasian foreigner. Ray was not allowed to be with me. It turned out to be a nineteen hour vigil. During the night, many women entered that room and delivered their babies.

Everyone had a cot to lie on that was about table height. It was hard and very uncomfortable. The idea to them was no one would be there but only for a brief time. No one was expected to remain nineteen hours!

I was amazed how the women remained so quiet until the child was born. If it was a girl, they screamed and cried loudly. I thought that they were crying because the baby may have been born dead or deformed in some way.

I asked the nurse, "Why are they crying? What's wrong?"

She responded, "Oh! It's another girl!"

The nurses came and went throughout the night. They checked on me and patted me on the arm and said, "No pain, no baby," and walked away. No medication was administered until the time of delivery.

The next morning at 8:50 a.m. our son came into this world. Once I was placed in a room at the hospital, visitors came to visit. The news spread quickly that it was a boy!

The Chinese believe that you receive favor from God if the first born is a boy. Even though we told them time and again that we would have been just as happy with a girl, they never believed us! This concept was so ingrained within their culture that it was hard for us to comprehend.

Two days later, an American lady was taken to the hospital and placed in a nearby room from me. She had been in an accident while visiting Malaysia. Her friend, another American, could be heard coming down the hallway calling out that something terrible had happened. Very clearly from my room, I could hear her voice tell of the assassination of President John F. Kennedy.

I remember the emotion I felt as I lay in the hospital bed trying to process how someone in America could kill our President. It was hard to comprehend! She came by my room to share what she knew. Many Chinese and Indian nurses came to my room and expressed their sympathy to me in the loss of my President. In fact, some of them even said, "our President." This was one of those tragic events that causes people to remember exactly where they were at the time they heard the news. John was only two days old.

Elizabeth Hale, a former missionary to China, who was serving in Alor Star, Malaysia, came from the mainland to Penang to visit us. Elizabeth braided her hair and pulled it around to circle her head. She was a true "Lottie Moon," showing her sacrificial love for those who had no one to care for them. She took the ferry and brought with her cans of Johnson's prickly heat baby powder. She brought eighteen cans in a burlap sack. She spent time with us, sharing what the Lord was doing in her life and ministry. She prayed for us and encouraged us as new missionaries. We will never forget what she said to us as she was leaving our home to return to her place of service.

"Remember this! You may bring many Indonesians and others to the Lord, but you must not fail with your son in bringing him to Christ." This dear lady was filled with the Holy Spirit and had the gift of wisdom. We kept in touch with each other long after our departure to Indonesia. Today, Elizabeth is enjoying her rewards in heaven and the fellowship among her many Chinese friends whom she loved so well.

Shortly after arriving home from the hospital, I began to run a high temperature. I developed a staph infection that began while I was a patient at the hospital. This was a very difficult time with a newborn and such a high temperature. Each day for seven days, I had a penicillin injection at the hospital.

During this time, Alice Chew wanted to introduce us to Malay and Indonesian food. She brought an array of morsels that she had made for us to try. Alice brought us a dish of black rice with grated coconut on top with thick coconut milk (*santan*) poured over it. It was interesting looking! We had been warned many times not to offend the people by not eating their food. We lifted our spoon slowly to our mouths and tasted this new concoction. I watched Ray's reaction as he watched mine, looking for reassurance from each other. Black rice with *santan* and grated fresh coconut became one of our favorites over the years.

We are grateful to Alice for taking the time to introduce us to foods that we most likely would not have ever tried had she not made the effort. When we arrived in Indonesia, we already knew which local cuisine was really good, all due to Alice's efforts.

Mary Oh was a faithful member at the Georgetown Baptist Church who came daily to teach me how to knit. Mary was an elderly, elegant lady with beautiful white hair that was pulled back in a French twist. She was a person who was gifted at handwork, and she always seemed to be working on making something for someone. Through our conversation, she found out that I did not know how to knit. She insisted on teaching me. Mary chose the yarn in charcoal grey and burgundy red which proved to be a good choice. She suggested I knit a sweater for John in a size three so he could wear it once we returned to America. I succeeded at knitting the front and the back and she did the sleeves. John wore it several times on our first furlough, and then I carefully packed it away. I was happy to give it to Christopher Ray, our grandson, so he could enjoy wearing this very "special" sweater. Now our second grandson, William, will wear it next. Hopefully, that sweater will be a part of our lives for many years to come because it represents a ministry of a lovely Chinese lady who was reaching out to me at a very significant time in my life. She endeavored to be "family" for me in her own way.

Visa Problems

All during our time in Penang, we worked toward getting a visa to Indonesia. After several months, we received word that our visa had been sent to the Indonesian Consulate in Penang. This was confirmed to Dr. Minor Davidson and Ray by the Consul over the weekend. They made an appointment at the Consulate that following Monday to have the visa placed in our passports. Over that weekend, the confrontation between Malaysia and Indonesia heated up, and the Indonesian government closed the Consulate. They took proof of our visa with them.

President Sukarno of Indonesia had been vehemently opposing the creation of Malaysia. He declared a *Konfrontasi* with Malaysia in January 1963. It was an intermittent battle over the future of the island of Borneo between British-backed Malaysia and Indonesia. This opposition went on for three or four years. Malaysia Day was declared on September 16, 1963. That was the weekend that the Indonesian Consulate closed.

This opened a whole new episode for us. Since diplomatic relations had been broken with Malaysia, we had to turn to Bangkok, Thailand, for help through our Baptist Mission office, which was working with the Indonesian Embassy in Bangkok. Through that office, several servants of the Lord assisted us until our visa was granted by the Indonesian Embassy in Bangkok. This included sending our passports through the mail (not too reliable) to secure the visa before the expiration date. Those were anxious days.

The members of the church wanted us to remain with them, saying that there was so much to do right among them. The Lord had given to us a great love for the people of the church. We had bonded well and had made many lasting friends. He had given to us a special assignment in Penang with memories we would take to our death. It was tempting to stay since we knew we were headed into a land with fewer amenities, and one which was also at war.

But the Lord had called us to Indonesia. We knew that we must be obedient and go where He wanted to place us. We knew He planned to use us in the largest Moslem country in the world.

It was the middle of January, 1964, when we received word from the Bangkok office that the visa was now in our passports. What a great relief! We had about one month to tie up our work in Penang and prepare for departure. Our entry to Indonesia would have to come through Bangkok rather than Malaysia due to the on-going political confrontation. John, our son, was three months old at the time of our departure.

One member wanted to know if we could use a footlocker as we had accumulated items while there. We agreed that it would be helpful and were grateful for their thoughtfulness. When they brought the "footlocker" over, it was a beautifully carved teak chest lined with camphor wood. Even today when we look at that chest in our home, it brings warm feelings about those dear friends in Penang.

On January 16, 1964, a few weeks before our departure we received a letter from Charles H. Morris, Chairman of the Malaya Baptist Mission who wrote the following text:

Dear Ray and Joyce:

As you are about to leave Penang for your chosen field of service I want to write to you officially on behalf of the mission. We are grateful to the Lord for allowing you to come and share your lives with us and the people of Malaysia for this short time. It is the feeling of many of us that you were God's choice for meeting a very difficult and perhaps would be tragic situation in the Georgetown Church. It may be true that you saved a church from splintering into pieces and perhaps total disintegration in its testimony and usefulness to Penang area.

As you go your way we want you to know that we are grateful for the great contribution you have made. We would have loved to claim and keep you for our own fellow co-workers, but we know that where God's finger points, you must follow. As you go, be assured of the continued deep and abiding interest of your fellow workers here. If any of us can ever be of any assistance to you please do not hesitate to call upon us.

On behalf of all of our mission, be assured of our prayers and our very best wishes as you go to Indonesia.

Always your friend in Christ, I am,
Sincerely yours,
Charles H. Morris, Chairman

We were never fully aware of any major problem among the folks until our ministry was almost ended. It was at that point when the chairman of the deacons said to Ray, "You have taught us how to love and forgive one another!" God knew what that church needed and had used us in our innocence. God is faithful!

On to Bangkok

The journey to our appointed country was about to begin. Each day, we spent time in prayer preparing our hearts for departure. The unknown was more intense having a little one with us. We were traveling as three for the first time in our married life. The folks at the Georgetown Baptist Church were now family, friends for life. It was hard leaving them. Tears were in their eyes as they saw us off, giving to us their blessing and promising prayer support. The spokesperson for the members said, "Don't forget us, and come back to see us when you can!" as we boarded the plane.

Our planned schedule kept us in Bangkok for three or four days, because we needed to enter from a neutral country due to the confrontation. When we entered the terminal in Bangkok, Max Alexander, business manager for the Bangkok Baptist Mission, welcomed us. This man had worked so hard for us to get our visa. It was an opportunity to thank in-person those missionaries who assisted us in securing our visa to Indonesia. They were the ones who worked through the Indonesian Embassy in Bangkok when the Indonesian Consulate had closed in Penang.

Also, it offered an opportunity to visit with JW and Alice Wilson. They were appointed with us. They were teaching at the seminary in Bangkok and were well underway studying the Thai language. The Wilsons had secured tickets to see the Thai dancers' command performance for the King and Queen of Thailand.

We were truly blessed to be in Bangkok at that particular time and to be able to attend this event with our friends. It was a once-in-a-life-time experience we will long remember.

Ray was taken to see the sites in the city the next day, which included the market on the river and the largest Buddha in Thailand. We rejoiced that we had been given the opportunity to see another place in Southeast Asia, to meet new friends, and to see old ones. It was a refreshing and great visit!

Arrival in Jakarta, Indonesia

It was evening when our plane landed in the capital city of Indonesia. The lights of Jakarta were off as air raids were taking place. We were told that kerosene lanterns were placed on the runway to help guide the planes. It was very humid, hot, and dark. What an introduction to our adopted country!

We discovered having John with us helped us clear customs quickly. The man standing next to me looked at our three month old and said, "Terus! Terus!" which meant, "Go on through."

People were scurrying here and there in the dimmed lights. Finally, after what seemed like a long time, but was only minutes, Leon and Anne Mitchell, and Stockwell and Darlene Sears came to welcome us. They had flashlights with them to guide us to the cars. We were directed to ride with the Mitchells. At that moment we felt relieved to be in the care of the missionaries. We arrived at the Mitchells' home after a short ride from the airport. Sue Meuth and Evelyn Swartz lived behind the Mitchells. They came over to greet us and we met the Sears and the Mitchell kids. Everyone enjoyed refreshments, and I remember the limeade was so refreshing that hot, humid night. Everyone was sharing information and enjoying talking and laughing together. There were many different strange sounds coming from the community where they lived. The numbers of people milling about on foot, bicycle, motorcycle, and in the *becaks* were overwhelming. We had finally arrived in our country of service! We stayed two days in the capital and then flew to Bandung where we would study the language.

Language School in Bandung
February, 1964

Bandung was known as the "city of flowers." This would be our home for the next year while we studied the Indonesian language.

We had received word just before leaving Penang to bring a large kettle so we could boil our water for drinking. When we got off the plane in Bandung, we were carrying a white wicker basket with our son, John, asleep inside, and our large kettle. Even today, some of our friends remember our arriving with that huge kettle and white baby basket. Several were there to meet us and welcome us to what would be our home for the next ten months.

The weather was cooler in Bandung, due to a higher altitude. Our house was located on a hill with three other houses that were built by Lottie Moon funds. We were excited to be living next to three other mission families.

Elinor and Wayne Pennell were our next door neighbors. They had completed their formal language study and were preparing to move to central Java for their first assignment in evangelism and church planting. Our other neighbors were John and Mary Nance, whom we had met in Singapore, and Bill and Dellanna O'Brien. The O'Briens had a son who was nineteen days older than John.

During our time in language school, John and Nell Smith, Shirley and Avery Willis, and Bob and Barbara Smith arrived to study the language. The Nances moved to Surabaya to serve in evangelism and church planting, and the O'Briens' assignment was to the Baptist Seminary in Semarang to teach music.

A real bond is formed with those who are in language school together. We all are called for the same purpose, and we all experience some of the same adjustments of culture shock, such as new language, new sounds, sights and smells. It has a way of unifying the group. This is why you may hear missionaries say that they feel as close or closer to their colleagues than family. When we meet with one another, regardless of the number of years it may have been, it is as if we have never been apart.

Studying any language is difficult, but even more so when outside tension and pressure is beyond one's control. Each day as we attempted to move forward to carry out our calling, air raids, sirens, and blackouts were a part of our day. There were times when we wondered if we would be allowed to stay.

A battalion of soldiers were stationed in a camp at the top of the hill on our street. Each morning they came down the hill to go through their drills. It became a natural scene to see them run, jump in the ditch in front of our house, and practice pointing their guns in our direction.

The house we were living in had a large picture window where our dining table was placed. We ate breakfast there each morning, and it became a normal routine to see the men pointing their guns while we ate breakfast. After becoming accustomed to us, and we to them, some of them would actually wave at us while pointing their guns.

Other Americans were talking about leaving, and we were just getting started. To others it probably looked foolish to be preparing for ministry, learning the language, putting our children in danger, but it made a lot of sense to us. We were where the Lord had placed us! It is actually good that we don't know what each day will bring. We just trusted our Father who promises He will be with us always. Each day we laid before our Father our needs for His power, His wisdom, His strength, and His boldness. We learned early that we would have to practice praying "without ceasing."

Four families had to share the use of one car. It was a small red car that often acted as if it had hiccups while trying to move down the road. We took turns using the car, and another family was always with us as we made our weekly trip to purchase our supplies. Once we turned off our street onto the street leading to the store, the car started hiccupping and usually paused after each hiccup. We learned to just go with the car's peculiar running. It got us there and back home. The whole idea was to be flexible and not be surprised at anything that happened. It was a lot better to laugh a lot, rather than get uptight and complain. Our ride in the car each week gave us a hearty laugh, which we looked forward to and needed.

The language teachers came to our house. A language school driver brought the teachers to us each day. Several came at the same time, and the teachers would switch students every hour. Mr. Markanda, an Indonesian teacher, taught Ray an hour each day, Monday through Friday. He suffered with gout and complained a lot. He was always looking for his glass of tea to drink as he came into the room. He enjoyed talking about himself. Ray learned a lot of medical terms with him because of his illness.

All the women had Miss Laksamini. She was a petite lady who was very prim and proper. She had never married and had taught school for many years. Her speaking ability was not as good as her comprehension of English. It was difficult to understand what she said at times. On one occasion, I was sharing with her that we were going up to Lembang, a mountain resort, for a picnic together. It had hot springs, vegetable fields, and fields of flowers that were harvested and sold to local markets. I asked her if we could buy some roses. She responded, "Yes, and you can get the stem too!" To her it made complete sense as so many Indonesians would buy only the flower petals to offer as sacrifices.

A young Chinese woman in her first years of teaching was one of my teachers. She never allowed us to talk without making corrections. Once she finished with our lessons, we felt as if we had been plowing the oxen in the fields all day. However, we made great progress under her, and that was the purpose of it all.

Ray was given an opportunity to preach his first sermon after only eight months in language school. A Dutch-speaking Chinese Indonesian taught Ray Biblical terms and the vocabulary of the Indonesian Bible. He helped Ray with his message and made corrections as he practiced. We were so proud of his bringing a message in the Indonesian language. The folks at the church said they understood everything he said. While the Indonesians were encouraging, they never missed an opportunity to offer criticism or correct us when we spoke their language.

There were times when we made colossal mistakes in our speaking. Oh! How we enjoyed each other's mistakes.

What great laughs we had! There are many words in the language that are similar in sound. They look and sound the same to a beginner. Often we got them mixed up and said the wrong one. The word for *neck* is *leher* and the word for *birth* is *lahir*. One of our men thought he was telling the folks that he had a sore throat when he really said that he didn't feel well because he had given birth!

The word for *prayer* is *doa* and the word for *sin* is *dosa*. We all fell out laughing when one of our missionaries said they should bring the entire family together and "sin" each morning. He thought he was using the word for *prayer*. Without doubt, we were entertainment for the nationals. They would bend over laughing.

The word for *donkey* is *keledai* and the word for *soybean* is *kedelai*. It was just what we all needed to have Mary riding on a soybean in the Christmas story. We finally learned to speak, sing, and write in the language with the help of the Holy Spirit and God's grace. I will never forget the day that I became consciously aware that I was no longer translating English into Indonesian in my mind but was actually thinking in the Indonesian language.

At the end of ten months in language study, the mission requested us to move to our first assignment. Our missionary friends from the Carolinas, Clarence and Ruth Griffin, were stationed in Central Java and were ready to take their first furlough, but they needed a replacement. We were assigned to Surakarta, also known as Solo, a city in Central Java.

Assignment to Solo in Central Java

We moved in January, 1965, to a rented house in Solo. Our friends, the Griffins, would be leaving for their furlough in a few months. Upon their departure for furlough, we would move into the mission-owned house that had been built with Lottie Moon offerings. We were delighted to become acquainted with the work by working beside the Griffins for that brief period.

At that time, five major Baptist churches and several preaching points (chapels) were established and growing. All but two of the church pastors were Indonesian seminary students. The other two pastors had completed their training and were married with families. Our responsibility was to serve the area, working with all the churches, coordinating programs, preaching, teaching, developing evangelistic projects, and helping to distribute the necessary funds for the work. Endless opportunities to witness and disciple others were part of a normal day's routine. Living in the community with the people gave numerous opportunities to share our faith with them.

When the pastor of the oldest organized church in Solo was called to another church, the congregation called Ray to be their interim while they searched for another pastor.

During this time, the economy was in great decline. Many people were hungry and didn't have basic necessities. There was a great deal of unrest and lots of demonstrations. The conflict with Malaysia still dragged on, but most Indonesians in our area were not aware of what was happening politically. When people started holding public meetings that were tilted toward communism, we began to see a change in attitudes among the people in the community. Many felt that communism could co-exist with their principles laid out in the *Pancacila,* which included nationalism, humanitarianism, representative government, social justice and belief in God.

The leader at the time, President Sukarno, had formed NASAKOM which stood for Nationalism, Agama (religion), and Communism. Signs went up everywhere with the acrostic NASAKOM. The people were learning through this new theme the three could possibly co-exist together. This political movement generated a daily routine of parades, banners, signs, and speeches, all advocating communism as the way to the future in Indonesia.

The spread of communism was part of a global movement at that time. China was the largest communist country, and it looked as if Indonesia was fast becoming the second. The Vietnam War was waging. There was an arms race between the United States and Russia, and Cuba was controlled by a communist dictator.

We had many prayer meetings among the Christians to pray that communism would not be allowed to take over the country of Indonesia. Some Indonesian Christians didn't think it was a threat and thought that it might help in some way. They were falling for the propaganda that they heard daily on the radio and read in the newspaper. We prayed daily that God would intervene on behalf of this great nation and that its people would be spared. It became increasingly more dangerous each passing week.

The weekly visit to the market to purchase vegetables, fruit, and meat, etc., was not an easy task. Everywhere we went we were watched. I learned to focus on where I was going and not to look at the people in the crowd during this time. On one occasion as I entered the large market that was a city block long, a man started following me. The building was similar to a large warehouse with a second level. The second level was built with a balcony design and one could look directly down on the open floor. They sold fish and other meats on this second level. As I entered, I saw the Javanese lady near the door who usually helped me when I would come to the market. She carried my large basket for me as I shopped. This man stood off from me on the balcony level, but when I reached the ground level he came up behind me. I could see everyone nearby was nervous. It was not unusual for people to stare, but I knew this was different. I was praying silently that God would protect me and give me wisdom to handle the situation. The man said to me from behind, "Dari mana?" which means, "Where are you from?"

I did not answer, but after he questioned me the second time, I said, "From Solo!" Solo was the name of the city.

Then he moved over to my side and said, "No! No! Asal dari mana?" meaning, "Where do you originate from?"

As I gathered my vegetables and bargained with the woman, I didn't answer him. The woman was extremely anxious. I even felt concerned for her. The conversations and noise level all seemed to halt, and the place around me became quiet.

He asked me once again, "Asal dari mana?" and then he started naming countries such as Poland, and Russia, but he knew, and everyone else knew, that I was from America. People from some of the communist satellite countries were very popular with the locals during those days. There were several families on military contracts from Russia and Poland. Ray and I were the only two Americans in the entire city of 2.5 million people. It was not popular to be from America.

His intent seemed to be to get me to say, "America" which would have given him freedom to take another aggressive step.

I prayed, "Lord, what should I say? I'm not ashamed of where I am from, but I need your protection now."

The Lord spoke to me so clearly, "Tell him that you originate from me!"

I looked directly at the man and said very clearly, "Saya asal dari Tuhan Allah!"

He was so startled by my declaration that he backed off, turned, and left quickly.

Many held their thumbs up in the air as I breathed a sigh of relief. I went away from that market more aware than ever that my Lord was with me as he had said, "Lo, I am with you always, even unto the ends of the earth" (Matt.28:20b).

Each day brought us closer and closer to a country headed straight for a full, communist-platform government. We knew our days there might be limited. Many organizations were told to leave. Our Baptist Mission was staying. As we saw all the aid organizations, contract teams, and the Peace Corp leave the country, we stayed, continuing our work, knowing we would be limited in what we could do during those turbulent days.

Coup d'etat

September 30, 1965 - a day we will not forget. We were up early to drive over to visit our friends, John and Nell Smith. They lived in Jogyakarta, which was about one-and-a-half hour drive from Solo. Solo and Jogya were known as the cultural centers of Indonesia.

While we were visiting with them, their gardener came to the door saying, "Something is happening in Jakarta!" John immediately turned on the radio to hear the news. We heard that a coup had taken place in the capital city of Jakarta. They reported that six generals were taken by a group of communist rebels during the night. The city was under the control of the communist party at the time of the broadcast.

We were concerned about what we needed to do at that point. Should we continue our visit with our friends or return immediately to our home? Only a few people knew where we were that day. We decided that we had to return to our appointed place of service and be with our Indonesian friends.

In our city of Solo, many of the communist leaders were staying with our mayor who was a communist supporter. The mayor's house was located about three city blocks from our home location. For several weeks, our city was under the control of the communists.

The heart of the shopping district was torched by the communist youth front. Most of the main shopping district was owned by the Chinese Indonesians, and the youth front was anti-Chinese.

Parades were held daily. On one occasion, we couldn't get across the main thoroughfare to our church. Even though our church was located close by our home, we had to cross over a main street that led through the city. We could not turn in the direction of the church. We decided to go toward the city and then cut off on a side road that would take us back toward the church. Trying to get in that position, we found ourselves at the front of the parade with uniformed young men and women carrying banners, drums, and communist flags. There we were, leading the way by coincidence, not choice. Because the parade was right behind us, many were waving at us! It would have been funny had it not been so dangerous. Our vehicle was a granny-apple green color, which stood out in normal settings. Envision two white Americans driving an apple green vehicle right in front of a communist parade! After several real nervous moments, we were able to turn off that main road and find our way to the church.

Cars overturned and burned, houses looted, and people robbed became the routine action of the day. We were restricted to our home after a curfew was imposed on the city. People were not even allowed in their front yards after 5:30 each afternoon.

Our Indonesian helper made a daily trip to the local market to purchase fresh vegetables and fruit. We were confined inside our home until Sunday morning. We were allowed to attend the Sunday morning services. Usually Ray preached in the morning service, but all afternoon and evening services were cancelled.

One morning, during this unusual time, two men dressed as Indonesian soldiers came to our front door. They both were around the same height. One seemed more nervous than the other. I was standing beside Ray, holding John in my arms. They had weapons and pushed their way into our house. They said, "The military needs your vehicle." Yes, the granny smith apple green Volkswagen microbus!

"Give us the keys!" they demanded, "We're in a hurry."

We had been warned that people were taking things from homes saying they were for the military. Later, I learned that Ray was praying silently just as I was, asking for wisdom as to how we should handle the situation. Ray was very calm. He told the two men who were holding guns aimed directly at us that the car we had in our possession was not ours but was given for the work of our Lord (Allah). He told them he did not have the authority to release the car to them. They became anxious and talked briefly to each other in Javanese. They turned and held the guns higher and demanded that we turn over the keys to them. Once again Ray told them that he was a steward of the car that was used for the work of Allah. They actually backed out the door and left the house. We were truly amazed! It was so clear that God's presence was with us that day. Our Father told Ray what to say and kept us calm in the midst of that storm.

They left our house and went to our neighbor's house behind us and took their vehicle. Our neighbors had a small car. Two days later, it was found on the side of the road to Semarang completely totaled.

We eventually learned that as a part of the coup, several of the country's top ranking generals had been brutally tortured and murdered. Their bodies were mutilated and thrown into an abandoned well. In Indonesia, there was widespread support for military heroes. When the news circulated throughout the country what had happened to these generals, the people turned against those who embraced communist beliefs. A nation-wide purge against the communist took place. Throughout the island of Java, communist sympathizers were murdered in great number.

General Suharto found out what was happening, and he rallied his troops to retake the city of Jakarta. The news that the city had been retaken by the military emboldened the military in other parts of the country. When the military entered Solo to clean out the city from the rebels, many were arrested from the communist youth front. The jails were full, and folks from the community were feeding the prisoners.

The police notified our church they were holding a young man who was a member of our church. He had been very faithful in attendance and was a leader among the young people. The police said they would release him to the custody of the church members, as they did not have enough room for all who had been arrested. Arrangements were made for the church members to go to the prison and inform the young man. He was required to sign papers taking responsibility for his actions. The church agreed to reorient him if he agreed to reorientation and expressed remorse for his mistakes and actions against the country. A group of four members were sent to the prison to hear him pledge his willingness to be released in the care of the church. The members were excited about securing his release. He had managed to win the hearts and minds of the folks at the church. He was tall, nice looking in appearance, and a very likeable person.

Instead of hearing words of remorse and regret for what he had done, they heard him say, "I will never deny my beliefs as a communist. I will gladly die as a communist!" He laughed at the church members. He scoffed and said, "The only reason I was in your church was to spy on you and report anything the American couple might say concerning the communist movement in Indonesia."

The members came back to report to the church what had transpired at the prison. They were visibly shaken over his response. One of the members stated, "Our convictions about Christ should be as strong as this young man's passion for communism."

We never heard what happened to him but fully believe he was killed. The members had prayed that he would repent and turn to Christ.

Ray and I were so glad we had been careful not to speak about political issues while we were at the church. We understood that we could not be sure about each individual person.

Ordered to Semarang

Looking out the living room window one morning during those eventful but critical days, two military police drove up in a jeep in front of our house.

I immediately noticed they were wearing white gloves. Their uniforms were crisp, freshly washed and ironed. My heart skipped a few beats as I went to the door. "What now?!?" I wondered.

We greeted each other and one of the men asked to speak to Ray. When Ray came to the door, they informed him, "You are ordered to go to Semarang." We had many questions for them, but the most important was, "Who is ordering us to go and why?"

He responded, "We are only bringing the message which was given by the police. You must leave immediately as the roads are now cleared. If you wait later in the afternoon, you may need a military escort!" Once again he urged that we try to leave immediately. "Communist rebels are cutting down trees on the road and blocking traffic to rob the people and take their vehicles," was added information he gave us that conveyed the urgency of the matter.

We thanked them and said, "We will leave as quickly as we can!"

After they drove away, we looked at each other with a lot of anxious thoughts. The big question was, "What do we do first?" I raced to get the suitcases and began to pack some items. Our helper who lived in the home was also nervous and anxious.

Ray rushed to see if we had enough gas in the car to make the trip. It usually took about two and a half hours by car from Solo to Semarang. We had made it a practice to have a full, ten-gallon can of gasoline on-hand in the event we could not buy gas, which often happened.

We wondered aloud if something had happened in Semarang. Our Baptist Seminary was located in Semarang, and there were five missionary units living there.

"Could it be that we have been requested to leave the country?"

"Have any of our missionary friends been abducted or put in prison, or even killed?"

These were only a fraction of our thoughts that day.

We called our helper who lived in the home. We shared with her all we knew about the situation. As Ray led in prayer we held hands together. We told her that we would return as quickly as possible, and if we were delayed that she would be informed by the police as to our circumstances. We rode away, not knowing if we would return or not.

We established a record that day in the length of time it took to reach Semarang from Solo. We made the trip in only one-and-a-half hours, a trip that normally took well over two hours, and sometimes three. The road was completely free of traffic, which was something we had never witnessed before.

Upon our arrival in the city, we stopped at the nearest missionary residence. Bill and Dellanna O'Brien greeted us. We shared with them what had happened. Bill revealed to us they had heard the news coming out of Solo and had been deeply concerned for our welfare and safety. The missionaries thought that we would be safer with them rather than being alone in Solo.

We quickly realized we were not as fearful for our own safety as they were. We were by ourselves and did not know the full danger. They had each other to feed news back and forth to, and the more they heard, the more fearful they became for us. We will always be grateful for their concern.

Dr. Ebbie and Donna Smith had extended an invitation for us to stay in their home. It was very touching for us to know how concerned they were for us. Yet at the same time we felt we needed to be where the Lord had assigned us. We struggled and prayed most of that night about what we should do. We see-sawed back and forth with each other about the pros and cons of the situation.

"I have duties and responsibilities!" Ray said.

I chimed in, "John would enjoy staying and playing with the kids."

Ray responded, "Our helper is anxious and fearful."

A missionary house was available, as one was on furlough at the time. The mission had offered that house to us to stay until the danger subsided if we desired.

Early that morning we received the peace and assurance we needed that the Lord wanted us to return to Solo. It was important we let the people in our churches know we were there with them.

Needless to say, our colleagues were not happy with our decision to leave Semarang. This turned out to be a real test of faith and endurance. And we faced some things on the way home that further stretched our faith.

Before we departed from Semarang, Bill O'Brien brought to us a small card from the Adjutant Commander of the Semarang Police. He was a friend to Bill and wrote on his calling card a message that introduced Ray as his friend and requested protection and respect for our welfare. This card proved to be invaluable for us during those months of violence and confusion in the country. We still have the card, dated October 30, 1965. We will always be grateful to Bill for his thoughtfulness in securing that card for us.

As we were leaving the town limits of Semarang and entering the main road leading to Solo, a group of soldiers with their weapons stopped our van and boarded without permission.

Before driving off, Ray questioned them about their intentions, "Where are you going?"

One of the men said, "We want a ride to our military base near Salatiga. They inquired as to where we were going.

"Solo," we responded. We felt fairly comfortable with the situation, and we headed toward Salatiga, which is about fifty-two kilometers from Solo.

Upon reaching this town, Ray pulled to a stop and everyone got out except one man. We asked him, "Why are you staying? Don't you need to return to your base?"

He answered with an air of arrogance, "I will inform you when the time comes."

Because he had his weapon with him, we both were uneasy about this individual, and especially since our two year old son was with us. Ray asked, "What is your name and where are you from?"

He snapped out his name as if it was annoying to him. Then he inquired as to who we were. Ray pulled out that card he had been given and showed it to him. After reading it, he sat quietly.

We had been riding about twenty kilometers when he began asking personal questions about the happenings in the country. He sought our personal opinions.

We had been informed that many communist rebels were parading as soldiers and the public should be careful. Ray said, "We don't know much about it. We aren't involved in politics."

We talked quietly to each other and decided we would ask him again where he was going. If he didn't respond we would tell him that we would drop him at the next town. This we preceded to do, but he still would not answer.

Ray said to him, "I will stop at the next town and you can get out there!" There was complete silence.

Once we reached the town, we stopped at a local market and asked him to get out at that stop. We were delighted that he got out. He had the most amazing look on his face as if he could not believe we were actually standing up to him, even though he had the weapon. We told him good-bye and wished him well. When we drove off with him standing by the car, he held up his hand with a thumbs-up sign.

I said, "Look at that! He gave us a thumbs-up sign!" We could not believe that he was actually encouraging us at that point.

Just as we were feeling relief, we came upon a group of young men all dressed in black with red bandanas. They were widely known as the "Marhaen," a communist youth front organization. They were carrying weapons of long bamboo poles that were sharpened to a needle point on the ends. They typically placed poison on the tip of the points. Their method of fighting was to hit with the bamboo pole and then ram the point into the person to kill them. There were about twenty of them on the road that day. They were swinging their arms, carrying their poles. Our van had to move at a snail's pace behind them until they finally moved over to the sides of the road to allow our vehicle through. Our main concern at this point was their discovering who we were in the vehicle. We prayed for a covering over us that even if they looked they would not see three, white foreigners.

Gradually, we were able to move past them and continue the journey home. We could see in a field by the side of the road as we passed through the small village of Boyolali that a battle had taken place among those who were anti-communist and the rebels. They had stacked bodies on hand drawn carts. I wondered out loud to Ray, "Wonder what else we will face before we reach our home?" We had about fifteen more kilometers to go.

Ray felt he needed to report to the police that we were back in the city from Semarang. A curfew had been put in place overnight, and we did not know that it began at 5:30 in the afternoon. As Ray drove down the main street in the city, he became uneasy that there was no traffic. He arrived at the police station and was immediately informed that the curfew was on. They ordered him to return immediately to his house with the escort of a policeman.

As I unpacked our suitcases, I looked at what I had put in thinking we may not return. There were baby pictures of

John. Our silverware, some special wedding gifts we had received, and other items that I had deemed important. It was in the quietness of the moment that I felt under conviction, realizing that those items did not have the same appeal as they had prior to our trip to Semarang. God's abiding presence was more important.

Several weeks went by with our remaining inside our home. We went to Sunday morning worship. All afternoon and night meetings were cancelled. A small group ventured out on Sunday mornings to worship and to pray.

We became creative about things we could do in our home since we didn't have the freedom to go outside. We spent time praying, studying God's word, playing with John, cleaning out closets, drawers, rearranging things, and catching up on some reading. Ray decided that he would paint his scooter. It was old and needed a new paint job. He spent several days preparing the Vespa scooter for painting. He worked in the enclosed backyard. He spray painted it blue and redid all the silver chrome. It looked like a new scooter!

Shortly after that, someone broke into our garage and took the scooter. When we went inside the garage we saw that nothing else was taken. On the garage shelves we had large cans of Maxwell House Coffee that would have brought a great price on the market. We also had large cans of Blueband margarine (Indonesian brand) which the thief would have recognized. They only took our "new" looking Vespa scooter. When we went out into the front yard, we saw the scooter leaning by a tree. What they didn't know was the scooter had a mind of its own! There was a special way to crank it, and one of the gears didn't work. If the rider put it in gear, it would actually throw him like a bucking horse. The thief had obviously given up on it! I won't forget Ray's excitement as he called out to me, "Joyce, it's out here by the tree!" We were delighted to find it was no worse for the wear.

After the curfew was lifted and things began to settle down again, we were visited by two American reporters from two very prominent US newspapers. They came to our house accompanied by an Indonesian man who spoke English fairly well. We did not know him. They had met him at the hotel in which they were staying and brought him along as a translator for them when they spoke with Indonesians. He came inside our house with them to see and hear what we had to say.

The political environment was still not safe, especially for us. We were the only foreigners living in this city of over two million people. All other foreigners had left. Whatever we said could be reported by this Indonesian, and we would have been asked to leave the country. We knew that we had to get the message to these reporters without causing problems. I decided to invite one of them to the kitchen to help me with refreshments.

I looked at the one that was nearest me and said, "Would you mind helping me with some refreshments?" He jumped up immediately, following me to the kitchen. I explained, "I invited you to assist me so I could inform you that my husband and I are uncomfortable with your questions concerning the government and recent coup."

"Why is that?" he responded.

I explained that whatever we said could be reported by the Indonesian man to local Indonesian authorities. "Could you communicate this message to your friend without causing problems?" I inquired.

I went on to share our purpose for being in the country. "We are in this country for the sole purpose of introducing the Indonesians to Jesus Christ," I told him.

As I prepared the limeade drinks for us, he was interested in the kitchen. Looking at the kerosene stove that burned with a blue flame, the large water containers, and the pasteurizer, he asked questions about the kitchen and about how difficult it was to prepare meals.

Trying to get his attention back on course, I explained, "We were not involved in politics and did not interfere in matters of the government." I continued, "We kept our opinions to ourselves."

As he listened he questioned, "Can we write anything at all about you and your time here?" Once again I expressed our concern that it might cause our departure from the country.

He was amazed that we still wanted to be there!

I was completely relieved when he said that he understood.

After they finished their limeade, he spoke very softly to his friend, and they left the house without further questions. Upon leaving, he thanked me for the tour of the kitchen!

Almost two months passed by without seeing anyone from our mission or hearing from anyone. Then Joyce and Jim Carpenter stopped by to see us. They were able to bring us up-to-date on happenings in their area of Java. We were so happy to see them!

Occasionally, we did get a phone call from some of our colleagues, though the phone service was not working most of the time. One interesting call came from Edna Smith who was located in Kediri, East Java. She was calling us to give information for the folks in Semarang. They could talk with us in Solo but could not reach Semarang by phone. We did a lot of relaying of messages those days. Each time Edna started to share the news they wanted us to pass along to our friends in Semarang, the operator broke in and ordered us to speak Bahasa Indonesian or Bahasa Perancis (French). We were speaking Indonesian, but she kept breaking in making the same demand. We finally told her that we were speaking Indonesian. She continued to interrupt our conversation. We found this frustrating but funny. Thus we decided to speak English, and she stopped breaking in on the conversation. Maybe she thought we were speaking French!

Signs of Healing and Stability

Little by little, the military brought stability to our region. President Sukarno was forced to step down as the leader of the country because of his close involvement with the communist movement and his ties with communist China.

General Suharto was chosen as the President of Indonesia in 1966. He was chosen by the Parliament because of his intervention to retake Jakarta from the communist rebels.

The country began to see signs of healing from the great tragedies of the communist movement. We knew our Father was giving these people another opportunity to hear the gospel and another opportunity for a good future.

So along with the turmoil and tragedy came opportunities. This was an unprecedented time. People who once put their hopes in the communist party and their belief that life would be better under that system began to turn to Christ in great numbers. They followed Him in baptism. New preaching points and new churches began to spring up all across the island of Java. New areas were opening to the gospel that had been previously closed.

Two special nation-wide efforts that contributed to church growth were the Sunday School Campaign and the *Gehiba* evangelistic outreach. Study courses were held in every major city with guest teachers. We had a national pastor and one of our missionaries to stay with us for over a week in this outreach program.

Gehiba was launched by our mission and national Baptists all across the country. *Gehiba* means new life movement. The increase in membership would not have happened apart from this emphasis on starting new churches. A group of young men from Oklahoma came for this emphasis. They toured the island of Java entertaining the churches. Many young people answered by giving their lives to full-time ministry.

We worked with several students as they came and went from the seminary each week. They were given a stipend for their traveling expenses and for ministry. A plan had been put in place by the previous missionaries to get the churches to take over their expenses little by little. We continued that plan, encouraging the churches to contribute toward the expenses of their own seminary student-pastor. The churches were growing, and most of the congregations were low income people, but we knew that their faith would grow if they were obedient in giving their tithe and offerings. We knew that if the church members did not feel a sense of responsibility for the support of their ministry, the church would not grow.

The two campaigns were highly successful in terms of maturity among members, commitments, and many new believers.

A Big Flood

In March, 1966, following in the footsteps of the Coup d'etat of September 1965, our city of Solo came under the attack by the few communist rebels who remained on the loose. They broke the dikes in two places in the Solo river, causing massive flooding of the city. The water level rose as high as six to ten meters in the heart of the city. The area that was hit the hardest was the location where the post office, police headquarters, banks, public courts, Sultan Palace, public market, and many, many shops, churches, and Mosque were. Many people climbed on the roof tops of their houses or on buildings to escape the high water and destruction.

We were extremely fortunate that the water didn't reach our house. We could hear, *"Tolong saya"*- calls for help throughout the night. One of our youth pastors stayed on the top of a church twenty-four hours before being rescued. A helicopter came over and dropped life rafts out to the people. We even heard about a woman who gave birth on a roof top.

After the water receded, we were able to go to the areas to assess the damage and find out how we could assist the people. The destruction was incalculable. Hundreds of people drowned, houses and entire *kampongs* (villages) were wiped out, the carcasses of animals were everywhere. It was a sight we will not easily forget. Documents, important letters, money—all were destroyed. The rice shipment for the city was completely ruined.

Our first thoughts after seeing the destruction and suffering were, "How can we help?" Ray set out to organize efforts with the churches not hit by the flood. We attempted to help those who had lost everything. Boxes of food supplies, soap, towels, and other important items were assembled to drop off to the people in our congregations. Solo, our city, suffered a double dose of sorrow with the Coup, followed by the flood.

Prayer was our lifeline during those days. How blessed we were throughout the whole ordeal. We learned to breathe in and breathe out prayers, moment by moment. During those days we were so dependent upon the Lord that when we heard a message from the Father it was very clear to us. Our ability to discern people's spiritual needs was heightened through the Holy Spirit. We recognized in a new way how small and insignificant we really were and how awesome and powerful our God really was.

Ray had been given the invitation to bring a message to our mission at the annual mission meeting that July of 1966. He shared about some of our personal experiences in Solo over the previous year. He had read a funny story in a magazine that he decided to use. The story was about a town that had experienced a great flood. The neighbors had joined together to look over the situation. They noticed a hat going back and forth on the top of the water. They called attention to the strange sight and wondered why the hat kept going back and forth. One person said, "I remember farmer Jones said he was going to mow his lawn come hell or high water!" This brought laughter from our missionary colleagues, as they knew we had had a taste of both in those months.

A Time of Reflection

We saw great growth during those turbulent days of our first term. The Lord taught us many lessons. We had learned to live in another country, learned their language, their culture, had had our first and only child without family nearby to assist. We had gone through the confrontation (war) of Malaysia and Indonesia, had lived in a city of 2,000,000 as the only Americans, had experienced a coup, had seen hundreds of dead bodies, had been held at gun point. We had been confined to our home for two months, had experienced a flood up to the roof tops in our city, had ministered among people who had lost everything they owned. Yes, our faith was stretched and new growth was experienced in the Lord. There is a big difference in *knowing* that there is a promise and *experiencing* the promise. We *knew* that our Father said that He would be with us, but living through these trials we *felt* his presence with us.

In November of 1966, we received word that Ray's dad had suffered a stroke and was in a coma. It was almost impossible to get a telephone message through, but we did succeed on one occasion during that time. His dad passed away the last week of December. The cablegram took three weeks to reach us telling of his death. Only those who have experienced this can possibly know what it is like to receive news like this and not be able to be present or even talk with family members. We shared together, and I listened to Ray talk about his memories with his dad. Dr. Keith Parks sat down with Ray in Semarang at a meeting and shared his experiences. He was a comfort to Ray, and he shared an insight that since Ray did not have the opportunity to be at the funeral, he might not have complete closure until he visited his dad's graveside. This counsel was very helpful.

Returning to America

Time was fast approaching for our first furlough. We were looking forward to returning to the States. Preparation was made for our replacement in order for us to leave in May. We made the suggestion that our Mission consider placing a couple who could remain with the ministry in Solo for a four full years. Previously all personnel who had served in Solo were directly out of language school and could only be in place for around two to three years.

Elinor and Wayne Pennell returned from their furlough to serve in Solo for four years. This freed us to pack our things for storage and to prepare for our departure from Indonesia.

Saying good-bye Indonesian-style took a full month because of being honored by many farewell dinners. Usually a gift of Batik cloth was given as a farewell gift. Everyone had to be visited, and permission to leave was requested from each congregation.

We were assigned to return to Kediri in East Java after our furlough. The assignment was to serve as evangelist, church planter and outreach person from our Baptist Hospital.

We stopped in Tokyo on our way home. We found John some winter things and a pair of shoes. We went on to Alaska, and that is where we came through customs. The gentleman who received our passports looked at them and said, "I can tell you are coming from Asia as your passports have that faded look that only the humidity and heat can produce." After inspecting the passports, he looked up and said in a hearty voice, "Welcome Home to America!"

It was a special day when we landed down in Florence, SC, to introduce our son, John, to his large extended family. A crowd of folks on a Sunday afternoon had made their way to the airport to welcome us home. John wanted to know if it was a *rapat* (meeting) because anytime there had been a large crowd of missionaries together it was always a *rapat*.

The year went by quickly with many speaking and sharing opportunities. John enjoyed going to kindergarten, discovering grandparents, and other family members. We moved twice during this furlough, finding it difficult to find a furnished place. Ray served our church as an interim pastor for our final five months.

Part 3

The Kediri Years

Island of Java

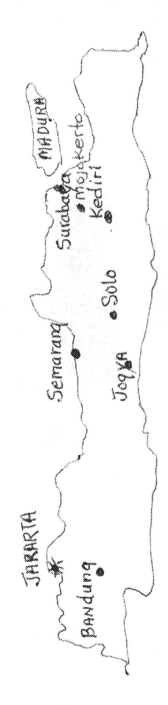

Assigned to Kediri, Indonesia

"...for the Lord your God is with you wherever you go."
Joshua 1:9

Kediri is located near the Brantas River in the province of East Java on the island of Java in Indonesia. The city is a major trade center for the Indonesian sugar industry. It is also the location of our Baptist Hospital.

Solo, our home city for our first term, was a larger city than Kediri. Kediri has more of a rural village setting, whereas Solo was a major cultural center in Central Java. The big difference for us between living in Solo and Kediri was the mission personnel. We were the only family assigned to Solo; we would join sixteen missionaries and eighteen kids in Kediri.

There were two compounds for mission housing located near the hospital. Most of our mission personnel lived in those compounds. We lived closer to the city center in a house located beside one of our Baptist churches, about a mile and a half from the hospital. Our assignment in Kediri was church planting and evangelism outreach from the hospital.

We arrived in Kediri in June 1968. This gave us a brief period to get settled in before school started.

School Days

One of my major responsibilities was teaching school. Classrooms were set up on the side of a large storage building. John and I traveled each day, Monday thru Friday, to the school building located near the hospital.

Located in the back of one of the houses was a playhouse built from cement blocks. Since all the classroom space was occupied, kindergarten was held in this playhouse. All the children were being taught by their moms or another missionary mom, and I taught kindergarten that first year.

Along with our son, John, were two precious little girls, Carolyn Jean Carpenter and Para Mullins. Their dads were medical missionaries working at our hospital.

Even though I had the responsibility to make learning an interesting experience for them, they often entertained me. John made a comment right in the middle of a lesson one day about Carolyn's hair. She had a head full of golden ringlets. Para had short straight hair that was like black velvet.

John said to Para, "Look at those tiny little curls! They are so pretty!"

Para responded, "I don't care. After all, they (the curls) belong to the mission anyway!"

Everything belonged to the mission...cars, houses, most of our equipment, etc., so why not Carolyn's hair, also!

On another occasion, we were having a science lesson about a cricket. We had a drawing of one, but my efforts to find one for a live demonstration did not succeed. I told them I had looked for one. While we were talking about it, to our great surprise, a cricket actually jumped up on the table where we were sitting.

Carolyn commented, "He heard us talking about him!" The kids were so excited to see the cricket that they scared him away. Seeing those moments through the eyes of a missionary child made life interesting.

Freight from the States

We had been in Kediri a couple of months when we were notified our freight had arrived from the States. It had been cleared in customs in Jakarta and was being sent to us overland by truck to Kediri.

A few miles before reaching us, the truck was stopped for inspections. The driver's permit was not valid, so they detained the driver for several hours and questioned him about his cargo. When they discovered it was coming to an American in Kediri, they apparently thought it was an opportunity to receive a donation. Several of the policemen accompanied the truck into Kediri to our house. We were told the truck would arrive by afternoon, but it arrived around 8:00 that evening. We requested several men to be on-hand to help get the crates off the truck. We figured right away that something had gone amiss when we saw the police. The driver explained about the inspection, invalid permit, and thus the reason the police were along.

Before unloading the two large crates, the police began their inquiry. "What is inside these crates?" questioned the policeman who seemed to be in charge.

Ray responded, "We have a complete list of items inside the crates. You are welcome to see it."

After glancing over the list, he insisted, "You must open them now!" Then he blurted out, "Do you have weapons in these crates?"

"No, we do not have weapons! We have never owned a weapon of any kind," Ray quickly responded.

It was close to 11:00 p.m. by the time the crates were taken off the truck. The men who helped unload the crates were tired and ready to go home. It would have taken at least two more hours to cut the bands, loosen the nails, and open the wooden crates. When the policeman saw it would not happen that night, he asked for a donation for the police, and then they departed. We felt exhausted by this time and were thankful it was over and had ended fairly well.

Village *(desa)* Ministry

A *desa* program began in 1966 as an outreach of the churches and the hospital in Kediri. It was led by a national pastor, Mulus Budianto, and a missionary, Mel Gentry. By 1968, they had opened work in eighteen villages. Ray was invited to work in this outreach ministry, as Mel was going on furlough and would be given a new assignment upon his return.

While getting settled into the area, Ray began working in outreach in the villages and following up with patients who had made a profession of faith in Christ while in the hospital. If they took the Bible they were given as a patient in the hospital home with them, this was a good sign that a follow-up visit would be accepted. So then a visit was made to the home. If they wanted Bible study and religious services, they visited the local *desa* leaders to get permission to hold the services in the person's home. Most of the leaders granted permission and welcomed them to that village. There were those who were more cautious and didn't grant permission upon the first request.

A team went along with Pastor Mulus and Ray to visit in the village before the service, inviting them to come to the service. Many came out of curiosity, and some came because of whose house the service was held. By the end of 1968, the *desa* program was growing and spreading rapidly into many villages and towns. There were over 500 believers who were being discipled. Many of these had already been baptized.

About this time, Pastor Mulus had gone on a trip and was returning to Kediri when the vehicle he was riding in had an accident. Mulus died shortly after the accident. This was a shock to the Christian community and a big loss in outreach evangelism. He was in his early thirties and left a wife and children.

Still, this ministry continued to grow, and many laymen began to take up the responsibility of pastoring these new congregations that met in the homes. They helped with the discipling of new believers and led the groups in services twice a month. We were delighted when the mission decided to ask Dr. Ebbie Smith to open a Bible School to implement training of lay pastors. He moved to Kediri in 1969 to begin this ministry.

As the laymen were able to take over the home groups that were established, Ray had the opportunity to explore new villages and new believers from the hospital ministry. He would be away most afternoons and return home late evening. He had to travel many kilometers to these villages, spend time visiting in the village, and conduct a service. By the time he returned home, it was late.

Even though this type of ministry was tiring physically, it was refreshing spiritually. It was a great joy watching new believers grow in their faith in Christ Jesus. There was a hunger for God's Word and a hunger for assurance of their salvation. A large majority were drawn to the knowledge that Christ would be with them in their daily lives while still on earth. They were able to see things differently and were having success in their new walk. They could see changes in their lives from day to day.

When Ray came home in the evening, I always asked him, "How did things go?" We took time to catch up with one another about what had happened during the day.

Ray came home from the *desa* one evening and shared that an elderly man was very ill, and some of the folks wanted Ray to visit him in the man's home. Ray continued sharing, "Two of the men went along with me. I witnessed to the man and asked him if he wanted to accept Christ as his Savior?"

Before he said, "Yes, I do" he asked Ray, "Why have you taken so long to come to me with this news? I could have had peace over the years if I had known this truth."

We reflected that evening on the millions who had not heard.

After living for nine months in a house across town from the hospital and school, we were invited to move to a vacant mission house. Ruth (Vandy) Vanderburg was leaving for her furlough, and she suggested that we move to her house to be closer to the school. We were delighted over this opportunity. This would give John an opportunity to be with the kids outside of the school setting. Ray and I could stop in for a visit with our colleagues without having to drive the car. I had not recovered from dengue fever and had very little energy to pack up again, but several in the station helped. We were pleased it worked out so well for us.

Vandy's dog had two puppies before she left, and she gave John one of them. He was a beautiful white Maltese. John said, "Let's name him Happy!" My mom and dad had a dog named Happy, and John liked him.

He said, "Grandmama said that if you named your dog 'Happy' then he will be happy!" So "Happy" it was!

Happy brought a lot of happiness over the years until someone took him from our backyard one night. John felt so bad, as he had forgotten to close the gate that evening when he was bringing something in the house. Later that night, someone came into the yard and took him. It was difficult for us, not knowing who took him or what had happened to him.

Winds of Revival

During the early seventies, winds of revival and spiritual awakening began to appear in various corners of the nation. We heard news coming from some of the outer islands of great miracles and great numbers turning to the Lord. In our own area, a group of missionaries gathered together for a prayer retreat at a mountain resort located at the foothills of Mount Merapi, a feared volcano by the Indonesians in Central Java. It was a refreshing treat for us to go into the mountain areas where it was cooler, and we had a place to walk and time to fellowship with one another away from our daily routine. Our missionary kid's camp was held at this same place each summer. It was a place we all enjoyed when we had the opportunity.

During this prayer time, individuals began to share or testify. Thoughts were revealed that normally would and should not be shared except out of repentance. A new found freedom swept over the group as various ones prayed, testified, shared burdens, repented, cried, and rejoiced over burdens being lifted. We were experiencing James 5:16,"Therefore confess your sins to each other and pray for each other so that you may be healed. The prayer of a righteous man is powerful and effective." It was evident that the power of the Holy Spirit had fallen on the group. It was a painful time, as well as a joyful time. I thought of how grateful I was to witness and experience this powerful encounter with the Holy Spirit.

The session started after our evening meal around 7:00 p.m. and ended after midnight, without anyone being aware of the time. I remember the great joy that we all shared. Hours passed by like minutes when we met to pray. Many began hearing about the prayer retreat that was unlike all others. Nationals wanted to speak to us about it. One pastor came all the way from Central Java for a visit so he could hear first-hand about what happened. He shared that he wanted the Holy Spirit to empower and control his life. Later he shared that he sat in the back of the bus on the way home and was able to look up at the stars. He asked God to forgive him and cleanse him and to empower his life for His glory while riding in the back of that bus!

Ray was elected moderator of the mission in 1970. The executive committee met in Jakarta. The committee had a devotional and a brief prayer time before handling the business of the mission. After this renewal experience, things were different. They began their meeting by prayer and they continued to pray. They prayed for a couple of hours that again seemed like minutes. They discovered that business was so much easier to conduct and took less time than usual. The winds of revival were moving among His people throughout the nation.

One day, Ray rode his scooter to deliver a letter to a pastor nearby our house. On the way back, at an intersection on a dirt road, a car came through and hit the scooter on the back-side, causing the scooter to go out of control. As a result Ray's right foot was broken. He was taken to the hospital in a matter of minutes. They fitted him with a cast, and he was told to go home and rest.

This turned out to be a perfect time for him to read, and pray, and spend time in God's Word. One of several books he read was Hannah Whitall Smith's *The Christian's Secret of a Happy Life*. All alone, reading God's Word, praying and singing, the Holy Spirit flooded the room with His presence. This was an encounter with God's power unlike and different from any other experience. Ray felt a warm touch all over his being. God gave him a fresh touch of His love and power and filled him with joy.

Fellowship in our Mission Station

Missionaries all belong to one big family. We may not always get along or agree with one another, but we still have a great love and respect for one another. Our kids refer to the adults as Aunt and Uncle. I never cease to be amazed over the relationship. It could be years since we've seen each other, and immediately upon meeting we can pick up as if we have never been separated.

In Kediri we had lots of guests. A small guest house located beside the hospital was always full, so most of us had guests for meals on a regular basis.

One year, Thanksgiving had come and gone, and we were in the early weeks of December. Each of us had had our share of company. We were all tired. Several of us were talking together when a person came exclaiming, "The Trees are coming!"

Laverne Applewhite replied emphatically, "Who are the Trees?"

Our first thoughts were, "Another guest!" It turns out, the trees we had ordered for Christmas had arrived on the truck. We laughed and were happy to know they were trees and not more guests.

Every Tuesday evening, we would rotate from house to house for our weekly prayer meeting. We called them "station meetings." This gave us the opportunity to sing in English, pray, and study God's Word. Also, we enjoyed the fellowship time.

We tried to make a special effort to get together for ice cream suppers at least once every month or so. Those would be held on a Saturday afternoon around 5:00 p.m. Everyone would bring a churn of ice cream and we tried not to duplicate the flavors. This was great fun, and all the adults and kids looked forward to those times.

Every Thanksgiving and Christmas we were all together. Each person contributed a dish or several dishes, and we ended up with a great feast. At one point we had as many as thirty-four in our fellowship.

Well known pastors, Southern Baptist leaders, and outstanding laymen would visit us in Kediri to see the hospital and meet the missionaries. We even enjoyed, on several occasions, having United States Ambassadors visit us.

For our recreation, most everyone played tennis and walked. A public swimming pool was accessible and the children occasionally went for an outing. Children played board games, but mostly played outside games they knew and Indonesian games they had learned. John and his friends set up a matchbox city under one of our trees. They had the gas station, bus station, hotel, school, church; they played for hours, driving around their matchbox cars through their set-up city. Television was available but the reception was poor, and there were hardly any programs in English.

Mission Survey, 1971

In the early seventies, our mission invited three men to conduct a thorough survey of our mission work and bring suggestions for the future. They were Dr. Cal Guy, Missions professor at Southwestern Baptist Theological Seminary in Fort Worth, Texas; Dr. Bryant Hicks, missions professor at Southern Baptist Theological Seminary in Louisville, Kentucky; and our own colleague, Dr. Ebbie Smith. Ray was serving as the moderator of the mission at this time. This gave him the opportunity to assist this team when they surveyed Kediri. The team worked for a couple of months gathering information, testimonies, opinions, and traveling across the entire island of Java and points in Sumatra. The results of the survey were presented at our annual mission meeting held at a mountain resort called Tretes near Surabaya.

The first full day was spent in worship, prayer, and praise. The adults met in a large meeting hall at the resort and the kids met in another place on the grounds. While the kids worshipped, they felt the Lord's presence. They left their meeting place and rushed into our meeting. Some of the older kids shared what they were experiencing. The entire mission family joined together in confession, prayer, and praise. A time of reconciliation and forgiveness took place among all in attendance. God's love overflowed in that meeting hall. The Lord was preparing us for what lay ahead.

Out of this survey came some monumental decisions that disturbed the status quo and caused families to make major adjustments in order to move forward in reaching the people for Christ. The major recommendation was to close the seminary program after those who were presently in seminary had graduated. The new program would be seminary training by-extension or programmed learning. This would begin immediately, even while the traditional program was still in place, which would later be phased out. The major reason for the change was to train and equip as many as possible to reach the masses. Even though we had over two hundred attending the seminary, we realized we could be training twice as many on the local scene where the people lived. Many from the villages wanted training but could not afford to move their families in order to study in a formal setting. One other reason was those who graduated from our seminary did not want to return to the village to minister. Most of the graduates wanted a ministry in the city. The new plan was to have an extension center within each large city where we already had missionary personnel assigned. That person would be responsible for the work in their city and surrounding region. Many of our missionaries and some pastors were invited to teach courses in the extension program. The seminary building would continue to be used in training pastors using the same method as taught by extension.

Several missionaries were assigned the task of writing the curriculum materials for the leadership training. As the courses were completed, study groups were set up all across the country. Often the missionary in charge could not keep up with the demands. Thus, he often enlisted missionaries assigned to evangelism and church planting to join in meeting the teaching demands when possible. Many of the missionary women helped with teaching some courses, including me.

At first, like with all organizational change, there was resistance. Some of the pastors and church leaders saw it as taking away something from them, rather than giving them a new avenue of reaching and training more people. Many felt their status was being weakened by opening up training outside the institutional confines to laymen.

Along with the recommendation of changes for the seminary came the recommendation that churches must become financially independent of the mission. This was true with the institutions as well. Some pastors' salaries were subsidized by the mission. Now, each church was to be evaluated according to her needs. A time-table was placed on that church to work toward becoming financially independent. At the end of that set time, a fresh look was given to the situation. A large number of our churches had been financially independent for several years. This would be set-up for the other churches to work toward financial independence. Some responded in a positive way and worked to achieve that goal with their churches. Others resented this action and chose to allow this action to be an obstacle for them.

Subsidy was necessary in the beginnings. It stimulated the start of a church, but along with it came many limitations. People began to look outside of their church body for aid, rather than applying God's principles of giving to support the storehouse. Over the years, I have seen a one-time gift of outside help boost and encourage the people, and I have seen outside donations of financial aid cripple and stifle growth. Permit me at this point to give a word of caution to those who would like to give a direct gift to a project on the field. For best results, it is always best to consult the mission personnel on the scene when giving financial aid. It is also important that the local people understand if it is a one-time gift so they will not expect regular contributions. The survey team felt that if we were going to require the Indonesians to make certain changes, then we as a mission should make changes also. The size of our houses would not exceed a certain square footage; they would be modest dwellings. The larger mission homes were built in the very early days of the work in the country. The houses had to serve the families that lived in them, but were also often the only place available for others to stay. In those earlier days, there were very few hotels. Families stayed in the homes of the missionary to attend meetings, conduct ministry, and visit. The home was also a school classroom for the children (all were home-schooled then). It was a place where pastors came to meet, to share food, and fellowship. The entire setting in those days was unlike what one would see today. As the country made progress economically, hotels and other places to stay were being built as well as restaurants. Public facilities were becoming available more and more. Earlier necessities had become less important, as the situation and needs were different now. Therefore, the missionary could consider a small dwelling, like unto those of their Indonesian neighbors at the time.

There was a call for scaling down in the transportation as well. Most of the people we ministered to lived in a village. They had a bicycle and a few owned motor scooters. Rarely did a family own a car. After a lot of praying and soul-searching, we decided to surrender our large micro-bus for a safari jeep. We felt this was the right move for us to make in regard to the village work.

Changes were gradually made over the years to identify with those in our community. This was done without jeopardizing the health and welfare of our own families.

Many lessons were learned along the way. It was easy to make decisions and to talk about changes, but implementing them was not as easy. There were some missionaries who did not follow through, but most put feet to their decisions. When God wants to make His move to lead His children, the devil tries so hard to divide, cause negative thoughts, and bring about a spirit of rebellion.

Dr. Cal Guy made the statement at the time of his presentation, "In making these changes some of you may wander in the desert for a while, or you can accept them in obedience and move forward." Over the next several years these changes gradually were implemented. Even though some were bitter and held resentment, the majority moved forward and began to see progress developing.

Even though there were strained relationships with a few of the national leaders, it did not filter down to the local level to hinder our work. Opportunities to witness and begin new work were unhindered for the most part.

One group stood out as an example of how the local congregation could build their own building. The new believers at Djaja Bakti in Karanganjar did just that! All the members and even local neighbors built their church building, even though they were low income farmers. They built the windows and doors at their homes. Once completed, they rang the village bell, telling people to come to the church to put them in place. Their first worship service in the completed building was one of great praise to the Lord. Their faith grew as a body of new believers as they worked together to build their house of worship.

Four years had gone by so quickly. It was time to prepare for our second furlough. The past four years had been full of unexpected turns in the road, but filled with many new experiences in the Lord. We felt that we had learned a lot of new lessons and experienced new growth in Him.

Long before we knew the term "prayer walking," we had been doing just that! Praying while, walking, working, eating or sleeping. The Lord was teaching us how to walk with Him.

Second Furlough

This furlough was again spent in Florence, SC. This meant we would be looking for a furnished place as we did the first furlough. This time we rented an apartment that had the kitchen appliances. We borrowed some furniture from friends and family.

Ray's home church, Sunset Park Baptist in Wilmington, North Carolina, furnished us a car during this furlough. Purchasing a car is always a huge expense for the missionary. When it's time to return to the field often times missionaries suffer a financial loss in sale of the car. Sunset Park blessed us beyond words through the use of a car while we were home in the states.

John entered the third grade. This was his first public school experience in the States. He came home the first day and told us that he saw two little girls who looked exactly alike, and they were twin sisters. He said, "I wish I had someone with me like that."

John accepted Christ as Savior during this furlough year and was baptized at the Calvary Baptist Church. He was comforted in that he was not alone because Christ was with him.

A unique blessing came in the form of a huge snow storm during our furlough. It was our first opportunity to play together as a family in the snow. We had mentioned to several that we wanted it to snow while we were home so John could experience seeing and playing in it. That February it started snowing, and it snowed for most of the day. One lady called, "You can stop praying now, we have

107

enough snow!" It was fun for John, even though the electricity went out.

How we managed all the speaking engagements, world mission conferences, camps, etc., while trying to have quality family time was a real test of fortitude and strength. We would say to each other that we needed to go back to get some rest, but furloughs were always like that, crammed full with so little time.

Third Term of Service
1973 – 1977

"And we know that all things work together for good to those who love God, to those who are the called according to His purpose" Romans 8:28

We had been reassigned to Kediri to continue in village evangelism and outreach. We were blessed to return to the same house.

John and I spent our weekdays in school. He had two other kids in his fourth grade class, which was taught by one of the missionary moms. I taught second grade, and seventh grade history. School started at 7:30 a.m. and was out by 1:00 p.m., with a thirty minute break at 10:00 a.m. I was given the opportunity to serve on the Education Committee in the mission, which gave support to the teaching moms.

John spent the afternoon doing homework and playing with the other children. I had lesson plans for school and taught English as a second language to the nurses at the hospital. Also, I had a group to come weekly from the community to study English conversation. Several times a week I attended meetings at my church, and I taught young people in Sunday School every Sunday. In Solo and in Kediri, I served in the women's ministry, both locally and for a while on the national level. Days were filled with many activities other than school. I joined Ray in outreach when I could.

Ray was the station Treasurer. He spent mornings in his office with those duties making preparation for his teaching sessions during the afternoons and evenings. He was with us for lunch, and then he would be off to various places for Bible studies, preaching services, and follow-up evangelism. We were ready for bed by the time he returned home.

Just as the missionary adults met weekly on Tuesdays for fellowship, prayer, and Bible study, we set up a time for the kids as well. The children met each Saturday afternoon for their English worship service. Different ones among the adults led the service. This gave to them an opportunity to worship in English. In addition to this, they attended Indonesian worship services, and Bible lessons were included in the school curriculum for each grade level as well.

We endeavored to keep Saturdays free for the family. This gave an opportunity to take a short trip or be at home with each other.

Ministry in Njadiredjo

Some of the medical staff at our hospital in Kediri told Ray a teenage boy was hit by a jeep on the road in front of his home about fifteen miles from the hospital. He was admitted to the hospital and the word was that he was lonely. His family was not with him. Ray visited Suroso and found a sixteen-year-old young man with a tender heart. Several of our medical personnel spoke with him about the Gospel. "May I share with you about Jesus Christ?" Ray requested.

Suroso's response was favorable. "Please, I want to hear more and more about what Christians believe."

Over a period of several days of Ray and others visiting him and sharing the good news, Suroso prayed to receive Jesus as his Savior.

Suroso's uncle, Pak Kaelan, came to visit him twice a week. Each time he visited his nephew, he noticed those who stopped in to check on Suroso prayed with him. They always closed their prayer in Jesus name.

Pak Kaelan asked his nephew, "Who is Jesus?" "Why are they praying in Jesus' name?" he questioned his nephew.

Suroso was nervous as he didn't know how his uncle would respond. He swallowed hard and began. "Uncle, I found out that religion is man's plan, but God sending Jesus was His plan! They read scripture to me that said the only way a person could be saved was through Jesus Christ, and when they invited me to pray to receive Jesus in my heart, I accepted!"

"Uncle, I have never felt such peace as I did when I asked Jesus into my heart and to forgive me of my sins. It is really true!"

This news was fascinating to Pak Kaelan. He was touched by the whole experience. His response was, "You bring home with you someone who could share with the family about Christ."

Ray went home with Suroso to meet Pak Kaelan's family. There were seven children in the Kaelan family, plus Suroso's family and other extended family. Mrs. Kaelen was a school teacher, and Pak Kaelan worked as a carpenter. Ray was introduced to aunts, uncles, grandparents, and neighbors. They all gathered together for this meeting.

"When would you like to begin Bible study?" Ray asked, thinking they wanted to set up a date and time.

Pak Kaelan replied, "Why not right now! We are all here!"

It happened to be a Tuesday afternoon around 4:00 p.m. For eight years Ray went faithfully every Tuesday at 4:00 p.m., to teach all who gathered in Kaelan's house. Ray taught them, verse by verse, most of the New Testament. As the weeks, months, and years passed, one by one they accepted Christ as Savior and Lord of life. The entire Kaelan family became believers, and many of their extended family and many neighbors found Christ as Savior. They established a Baptist Church and several preaching points/chapels as outreach from their church.

Lemani was an apprentice carpenter under Pak Kaelan's supervision. The apprentices stayed in the home for several weeks and then returned to their home. Each Tuesday, they were in attendance at Bible study. While teaching, Lemani raised his hand and said, "Pendeta, I believe!"

Ray stopped his teaching and led him in a sinner's prayer and everyone rejoiced. The following week he wasn't there. Upon inquiring we learned he had made the trip home to share with his family about his new found faith in Christ.

Ray invited me to make the trip with him to Lemani's village to see him and his family. Upon arrival to the village, Lemani met us with great joy and took us to his house where we met his mother, sister, and brother.

"Pendeta Rogers, I could not wait another day to share this wonderful news with my family." Lemani shared. "My brother has accepted Christ" he exclaimed excitedly. They all were delighted we had come. After sharing and praying with them, Lemani's sister also accepted Christ as her Savior. Lemani and his brother are faithful servants of the Lord even today. His brother was called to preach, and our last news was he was pastoring a church.

Suroso, the young sixteen year old, continued to grow in Christ. The Lord blessed him to complete his education from high school. He went on to college, and then to study in the University where he received several degrees and completed his doctorate. He is presently teaching in the University of Joygakarta, Indonesia. He has remained faithful to the Lord.

All decisions made while a patient in the hospital don't end as well as Suroso's story. A married middle-age woman had surgery at our hospital. She gladly accepted Christ after hearing what He had done for her. She prayed to accept Him in her heart. She was overflowing with great joy and agreed that Ray could come to her home to teach the scripture. Two

113

other ladies joined them in the study. He was successful with one visit, and then the second visit came. Her husband was present this time. Ray could tell he was angry, and his wife was very nervous.

He spoke, "Pendeta Rogers, I have not given permission for my wife to become a Christian!" He continued, "You will leave my house now and you are not welcome to return."

His wife sat quietly and cried.

Ray responded, "I will honor your request, but before I leave will you allow me to share with you what Christ has done for you?"

He gave permission but stopped him before he could finish. Ray requested, "May I pray for you and your wife before I leave?" He granted permission.

After the prayer, the woman said very softly as she told us good bye that she would read the Bible and continue to follow Christ in her heart. She said to Ray, "Please, please pray for my husband!"

These are the people who always remain in one's memory. We had no further contact with this family, but we were faithful to lift them to the Lord. We knew the seeds planted in this lady's heart would bring results in the lives of those around her in time. Over the years, we have trusted Paul's word in Philippians 2:12b-13 and have prayed that she "continued to work out her salvation with fear and trembling, as God worked in her to will and act according to his good purpose."

Man on a Bench

As Ray traveled to Trenggalek for a Bible study each week, he would often notice a man seated on a bench out front of a store. He promised himself several times that he would stop and speak to the man one day. It seemed that he was always in a hurry to get where he was going or in a hurry to get back home to Kediri before dark.

One day as he was passing by and saw the man seated on the bench, he waved to him and the man waved back. As he went on by, he felt the Holy Spirit saying, "Turn around and go sit by him." He turned around and greeted the man seated on the bench. "My name is Ray Rogers," he said as he approached this tall, large framed Chinese Indonesian.

"I am Tuan Teo," the man replied, reaching to return Ray's handshake. He was the owner of a store which sold a little of everything. It was something of a general store in the middle of the countryside several kilometers from the nearest town of Tulungagung. He invited Ray to sit with him on the bench. The usual questions began, "Where are you from? Where do you live? I see you pass by here often, where do you go?"

Ray explained who he was and what he did.

His response was, "I went to a Catholic school when I was a small boy."

Through their conversation Ray discovered that he had not embraced any religion. He and his wife practiced ancestral worship to some degree but didn't claim any particular religion. Ray asked permission to share his faith with him.

"Yes, I would like to hear what you believe!"

Ray took his Bible and opened the scripture, so Mr. Teo could see the verses as he read them to him. He paused after reading and explained the meaning. This was often interrupted by questions. They shared back and forth. Once Ray completed the full explanation of how one was saved, he asked Mr. Teo if he would like to pray to receive Christ as his Savior.

"Yes, I do!" he responded.

Together they prayed, having Mr. Teo repeat the prayer after him. This tall, large framed Chinese gentleman was like a tender child praying to receive Christ as Savior. Immediately, he wanted to go inside and share with his wife. Ray said he rushed inside and told her that he had prayed to receive Jesus Christ as his Savior. She smiled as she saw his excitement but looked perplexed all at the same time.

He invited Ray to stop by his place each week on his way to Trenggalek so he and his wife could study God's Word with Ray. Each week for several months Ray visited this couple, and she came to know the Lord. They invited in their neighbors to listen. They followed through with baptism and became members of the Tulungagung Baptist Church.

Mr. Teo said to Ray as we left Kediri several years later, "Pendeta (Pastor) Rogers if you had not stopped by my place that day, I probably would still be lost in sin with no hope." They rejoiced together that Ray had been obedient to the nudging of the Holy Spirit to stop and talk to the man on the bench.

A Time of Growth and Change

Going back as far as 1961, our mission formed a foundation known as a *Jajasan* that acted as a legal, holding-body for all properties purchased with funds from our board. It included Indonesian men in leadership as advisors. Later, a committee on Baptist Cooperative Work in Indonesia was established. This was a joint committee formed with members of the mission and Indonesian Baptist. This committee was designed to work together in all matters relating to Baptist work. It would be through this joint committee called "Badan Kerja-sama Kaum Baptis Indonesia" that the Indonesian Baptist Churches would form a convention.

Out of the changes implemented by the survey of the mission, the national leadership rose to the challenge to bring about a national convention. They worked toward organizing so they would be in charge of all Baptist work in their country. This was what was intended from the very beginning. We rejoiced over this action, but it came about a lot sooner as a result of the survey decisions.

The national convention came into being and took over the approval of missionary visas. Previously, we could go directly to government office and proceed with the renewal process, which took several weeks or months. Now, before we could begin at the government level, the leader of the National Baptist Convention had to submit a letter of recommendation stating that our service was still needed. Often the church leaders delayed giving their approval, making the whole process late. We found some waited until the last minute to assist the missionary. On one occasion

Ray was called to come to Jakarta to meet with them before they granted the needed letter.

When we heard that Ray was called to come to Jakarta, we became anxious and aggravated. As we discussed the matter, Ray added, "Why must I drop my work and arrange time to make a long trip? Don't they understand?"

We prayed as Ray prepared for this trip. Our prayer was that Ray would show forth Christ's love in his actions and words as he met with the national chairman.

He was called to give an explanation about the local government letter that had a whiteout and another date typed over it. He explained the dates were like that upon receipt of the letter in our possession. After making us feel as uncomfortable as possible, they then consented to grant the necessary letter.

We felt some of our brethren may have had some resentment toward Ray as he was the Moderator when major changes took place. *To us*, a moderator is the person who moderates the meeting and calls for decisions made by the body. *They* looked upon the person in-charge as one who could persuade others of a certain way because of his position.

On the local level, one of our pastors decided he would make things difficult for us. He met with Ray and told him he was not needed in Kediri. If he could not find somewhere to serve, he could just return to America!

Ray explained, "Pastor, I wish it was that easy! I can't leave until God tells me to leave!"

"Pastor, why do you say I am not needed?" he inquired.

"Our local pastors can handle the ministry outreach!" he replied.

"What about the thousands who are waiting to hear the good news in the villages? How can a few pastors reach these people?"

He didn't seem to have any ready answers to those questions.

Ray shared with him about his work and what he hoped to accomplish. He shared his call to missions with him and asked that they pray together. Ray said that he was interested in what he said about being called. In the weeks that ensued, this pastor seemed cool and distant. He never mentioned again that we should leave. When his first born son was circumcised, he called for Ray to come and pray for his family.

These were difficult days. As we were growing in understanding and having greater insight in local thinking, we prayed for patience. Our Father gave us the grace we needed to stand in difficult and uncertain times. We knew in our hearts that one day they would all rejoice over the course that was taken by our mission to reach the lost of their great country. We were beginning to see signs of growth and maturity, and we were also reminded that Satan would use whoever was available to him to do his bidding, be it a Christian or a non-believer.

The Lord used this whole experience to renew our call to missions. The adversity created in us a greater passion for lost souls. Later, we could see that it was good to have these trials so that our faith could increase and prove genuine and result in glory to our Father. But at the time I had to do some soul-searching. I had allowed myself to become bitter toward those who sought to do harm or get-even.

Ray kept saying, "We need to forgive and show them kindness."

I didn't want to show any kindness! "Where is their kindness?" I would respond. All I did was think of the injustice, ingratitude, and lack of kindness on their part.

One afternoon I got down on my knees beside my bed and told the Lord how I felt. I had done a fairly good job of putting up a defense against those who I felt had done us wrong. Then my patient, loving Father started showing me my sins. He showed me my anger, impatience, wrong attitude, self-righteousness, and my criticism. With a broken heart I prayed for His cleansing and forgiveness. When He was finished with me, I felt relieved, renewed, and cleansed. Along came answered prayer, and a true sense of His peace. In Hebrews 12:7 I was reminded, "Endure hardship as discipline; God is treating you as sons."

It was in later years that one of the pastors who had made it so difficult for some of our missionaries to renew their visa asked for forgiveness while he lay in the hospital. He told the missionary that was visiting him in the hospital that he "regretted" the way in which he treated them. This was encouraging to hear, even years later!

Third Furlough, 1977

We traveled home through Europe visiting Norway, Denmark, Belgium, Austria, and Switzerland. We arrived in New York in time to experience a blackout, which was very unsettling for our first night back in America. We managed to see several landmarks in the city, even without electricity. We wandered into an Italian family's restaurant, looking for something cold to drink. They found out it was our first visit to the city and that we were returning to America from Indonesia. They brought out plates of spaghetti, cold drinks, bread, and insisted we not pay. We were overwhelmed by their kindness to us.

Back in Florence, SC again, we found an apartment just one block away from the middle school where John would be attending eighth grade. Once again family and friends loaned us some furniture to use during that year.

During this furlough, we received training in Marriage Enrichment with the intention of conducting marriage enrichment seminars, which we were able to do on several occasions. We also had a two weeks training at the Clyde Narramore Clinic of Psychology in California. This brief course in counseling proved invaluable, especially in our later ministry in New Zealand, and other places.

John did well in school but found it hard to adjust to the eighth graders'emphasis on clothes and brand name jeans, etc. He was given an opportunity to work out of the school office one period each day. He enjoyed the opportunity to get to know his cousins and have fellowship with them during this furlough time.

We spent a week in Titusville, Florida at the Park Avenue Baptist Church, where the church staff along with pastor, Peter Lord, ministered to us as dry, thirsty missionaries. We were preparing our hearts and minds for the separation of our son from us in our next term of service. John would be entering high school and would go to the International High School in Jakarta. Cecil McGee, their educational minister, asked that we bring John for a weekend. It was wonderful! Cecil talked with him along with us and laid hands on John as he prayed. Cecil was a great encourager! We worshiped, prayed, and fellowshipped together that weekend. The folks at Park Avenue made it possible for us to have a VIP tour of Cape Canaveral.

We had a brief visit with Dr. Joe Pipkin and Catherine in Orlando. Joe and Catherine spent many summers in Kediri in the dental clinic, volunteering their time to make our dental clinic in the hospital the best it could be. We enjoyed Epcot and Disney World while there. On our way back to Florence, John said, "I feel a peace about it now. This weekend reminded me that I am not alone!"

On April 18, 1978, my dad, S. Mortimer Campbell, passed away. He had suffered a heart attack in August at the beginning of our furlough time and declined month by month after the heart attack. This gave my mom and us an opportunity to adjust and prepare for his homecoming with the Lord. We had many quality moments with him during those months. He was so concerned about mom and how she would cope.

While visiting a few weeks before his death, he and I went to Willow Creek Baptist church to the cemetery. As we walked together observing the place where his dad and mom, and my grandparents were buried, he showed me where he would be placed.

Trying not to become emotional I said, "Dad, tell me about what kind of service you would like when that day comes."

He mentioned some hymns, some scripture, and who he would like to conduct the funeral.

I expressed to him how much I loved and appreciated him.

It meant so much to him that we were at home during his time of illness. I was blessed to be present and was able to prepare the program for the funeral service. He was a wonderful father, who was an example to me of God's grace, kindness, and faithfulness throughout his life. I was indeed fortunate to have him as my father. Many people loved him and respected him; the huge turnout for his funeral proved it in a small way.

Fourth Term to Kediri

A new adjustment awaited us this term. We arrived back the last of June 1978. In August, we would be taking our son, John, to Jakarta to attend school.

A home for our missionary kids to live in while attending the International High School had been built near by the school several years earlier. A missionary couple had answered the call to be "parents" to these kids while they were in high school. Everyone living in the home was a child of our mission family.

We took John to Jakarta to help him set up his room and be with him during his first days of orientation. About ten kids John's age from our mission were entering the ninth grade along with him. His roommate was Jeff Lee, son of Carl and Twila Lee from Texas. They had been good friends for several years and were looking forward to rooming together.

While the crowd was off to the school, I spent some time in John's room. It was important to me to be in the space that my son would live, to pray over his bed where he would sleep, sit at his desk where he would study and work, see his clothes hanging in the closet. All the time I was trying to deal with my emotions and concerns for my young, thirteen year old son. I found myself writing some encouraging notes and scripture verses, placing them in his drawer, his shirt pockets, pants pockets so he would be encouraged upon discovering them at various times. He would be reminded that we were thinking and praying for him.

For the first time in thirteen years, Ray and I would be returning to our home in Kediri by ourselves. We would be over 500 miles away from him. Being in Jakarta, he would be at one end of the island, and we would be at the other end. We would see him again in December for the Christmas break. God gave us the strength and the courage we needed. A true test of faith and obedience are the most fitting words to describe that time in our lives. Only God, and those couples like us who have faced the same, understand.

The three of us huddled together to pray and say goodbye. Ray prayed a short prayer for us as a family. He reminded our Father that we had dedicated John to him when he was born and once again we were surrendering him to the Father's care and love. We were also grateful that he had a marvelous school to attend where he would have numerous opportunities for growth and development academically.

During this term of service, I was invited by the mission to serve as Education Coordinator. I served in this capacity for three years. The coordinator served as a contact person for the one-mom school to consult with when needed. Sarah Snell wrote the job description for the coordinator and served in that capacity to launch this new service ministry.

When I took the position, it was well organized. We published a newsletter each month with contributions from the children in the form of short stories, poems, etc. Ideas and tips were shared for various projects in the newsletter. It helped to serve as a link to moms teaching their children in the home.

Each school year, we brought all the children and their moms to the Baptist Seminary in Semarang for several days. We called it MK-Round Up. This provided a few days

125

of games, plays, contest, science fairs, and other activities to those one-mom schools. Standardized tests were given during this time together. It also gave to the moms an opportunity to discuss their concerns, learn from each other, see their kids in contests and plays, and have a break from the home-school classroom. This ministry was offered to me at a time when I could focus on the needs of others.

Our Home

Not having John at home, I had a new freedom for the first time in thirteen years; I would not be teaching school. Even though I had been very involved in the associational work and ministry in my church, I had not been actively involved in Ray's outreach ministry. Now I could assist him in his work.

We were able to begin several new groups working together. I taught all the children while he taught the adults. Each group was different and called for different and creative ways to help them grow in Christ. It was good for us both to be together working with the people, teaching, preaching, discipling, and witnessing. It was healing for us in the vacuum that was left when John went away to high school.

Our home was our special retreat from the hot, humid weather, and the masses of humanity that lived right around us. It was also a place where pastors came to share their heart; a place where people from the village could have a glass of hot tea or a cold drink of water, and many would have a meal; a place where folks from other regions could stay while receiving medical services.

From time to time, we had guests from America who wanted to see the ministry of the hospital, and they would stay with us in our home for several days. It was a place where needs were met emotionally and spiritually.

We invited a young girl from one of our mission families to come and study together with our other eighth graders in Kediri. Her mother had two other children to teach, and one was beginning the first grade. This would give to her an opportunity to get the two other children started in their routine. I supervised her work in Math and Science. She stayed over a month, and we enjoyed having a girl in our home.

Then a teenage Indonesian girl from my church became involved with a young man who was not a Christian. She was the oldest daughter of one of the leaders in the church. Her hair was long and curly, her complexion flawless, she had huge, sparkling black eyes. She was a beauty! Her mom and dad knew us well and had been in our home on many occasions. She had run off with this young man to spend time with him. His influence over her was causing her to be rebellious toward her parents. He was caught stealing while she was with him. He was arrested, and she would not leave the police station jail where he was detained. Her father came to us and requested that she come to our home since she would not return home. She agreed to come to our house. When it was time for her to leave the jail she threw a tantrum, and the police brought her to our house in the back of a truck with her feet tied. Upon their arrival, she was yelling and screaming for all the neighbors to see as they gathered by the hundreds to watch. Upon entering our house, she became quiet and was very respectful and well-mannered. She apparently had just wanted to put on a show to embarrass her parents.

It was extremely difficult to deal with her as the days went by. She revealed a dual personality which caused us to watch her every move. She requested to visit a former pastor's wife, saying she was seeking help from her. We took her to the home and visited with her for a brief time. We left her in the care of the pastor's wife for one hour.

Immediately upon our departure, she left the house and rushed out to the prison. Once seeing this young man again, she seemed emboldened and even more rebellious. We requested her to pray with us both morning and evening. We gave her counsel, read the word to her and discussed what we read, shared how making wrong decisions could ruin her life. I knew that she had made a decision and had been baptized. I asked her, "What does Jesus mean to you?"

She quickly said, "What do you mean?"

"How has he helped you in your daily walk?" I added.

It became evident she had never met Christ personally. She had joined the church and was baptized but did not know Him as her Lord and Savior. We asked her if she would be willing to pray for Christ to come and take control of her life? She agreed and knelt down with us and she prayed a prayer of repentance and acceptance of Christ. A change happened in her almost right away. When she left, we felt that she was on the right pathway. She went back to her home and her parents. She decided not to see the young man again. Several months later she was given an opportunity to leave Indonesia and work in Malaysia.

Two years passed when she dropped by for a visit. She brought an oil painting she had painted for us of yellow roses on black velvet. She shared how she was involved in a local Baptist church in Kuala Lumpur, Malaysia. She thanked us for investing time in her life and leading her to a personal relationship with Christ.

About a month later, John came home for Christmas from Jakarta. We had a big surprise for him when he arrived. Two Chinese ladies, whom we knew and often visited, invited us to select a puppy from their dog's litter. We missed having a dog after we lost Happy and agreed it was time to get one again. The puppies were mixed Pekingese and Pomeranian. We picked the one that untied Ray's shoe strings. He was a frisky, little, rusty-colored puppy with a Pekingese face and a Pomeranian plume-like tail. Ray brought the puppy out when John arrived home.

Smiling from ear to ear John asked, "What do you have there?" John took the little puppy in his hands and they bonded right then and there! Barney stayed with us for our remaining time in Indonesia. He was a fun dog.

Several months later, a man came to the front door collecting dog tax funds. Thinking that such a tax did not exist I enjoyed a few moments of fun with this "collector." Barney happened to be standing on his hind legs looking out the screen door along with me.

"There is no dog here!" I exclaimed.

"You have no dog?" as he allowed his eyes to move downward to Barney and then back on me.

Barney, of course, was doing his part by laughingly showing his tongue.

Then I said, "Oh, he doesn't think he is a dog! He thinks he is human!"

The man appeared amazed! "He really thinks he is human?" he repeated. I could see the breaking of a smile on his face. Then he said, "You tease me!"

We laughed together. I paid the tax and he gave me a receipt. He went away saying, "Lady, you make funny!"

The Little Boy

Most of these villages didn't have a road wide enough for a vehicle other than a scooter or bicycle. When Ray drove the jeep, he would park on the main road and then walk back into the village. Usually, Ray would drive the Jeep if the journey was over an hour. One time there had been a lot of rain, so as Ray headed off to a remote village, he felt it would be best to take the jeep. Normally, he would ride his Vespa scooter to this particular village because the scooter would take him right up to door of the family he would be visiting.

When Ray drove, a little nine or ten year old boy would always stay with the Jeep by the main road to make sure the mirrors and hubcaps, etc., would stay on the vehicle. He chose to do this for the *Pendeta* (pastor). He was a happy little boy who came running when he saw Ray in the Jeep.

Upon entering the village, Ray remembered that he did not have his flashlight with him, and it would be dark when he finished teaching. He proceeded on to the house where he taught God's Word to those who came that evening.

Immediately upon completion of the Bible study, the pressured kerosene lamp was extinguished and folks headed out quickly to their homes. The house where the Bible study was held was about a half mile from the location of the Jeep.

It was pitch dark. Ray immediately recognized his dilemma in not alerting the others that he would need help reaching the Jeep in the dark. He needed help in finding the path that led to the road. Searching he struggled to find his way and fell into the shallow ditch nearby the path, he

131

bumped into a tree, while praying silently that the Lord would help him find his way back to the main road and to his vehicle.

He felt someone come beside him. A little soft voice was heard saying, "Pendeta, take my hand and I will lead you out." The little boy who guarded the Jeep knew that something was wrong and came to find the *Pendeta*.

As this child led him to the Jeep, Ray knew that the Lord was showing him something significant through this little boy.

Upon reaching the Jeep and taking time to express appreciation to this little boy who had led him out of the darkness to safety, he headed home.

As he was driving along rethinking his experience, it was difficult to keep his emotions in tack. The Lord began to speak to him. He reminded Ray, He had sent him to Indonesia to do exactly what that little boy had done for him that evening. To one-by-one "bring people out of darkness into the light" and lead them safely home to the Father.

God used a little boy that night to assist a grown man who needed help in the dark, and to remind that same man of God's calling and faithfulness in his life. God's strength is truly made perfect in our weakness.

Graduation from High School, June 1982

All four years of John's high school years were at the International High School in Jakarta, Indonesia. Graduation Day was an exciting one. We rejoiced over how the Lord had cared for the three of us over those years. It had been a long four years!

At our mission meeting in July, we had a celebration for the twelve high school graduates. Ten of the graduates lived in the hostel together. Jerry and Bobbye Rankin were in charge of the program. Through poetic form, they presented a special tribute to each graduate. Special prayer was offered for them as they would leave Indonesia and return to America.

We were blessed to have Dr. Baker J. Cauthen that summer as our guest speaker. Dr. Cauthen had suffered a heart attack a few years prior to his trip and appeared frail and weak; however, his voice was strong, and he preached with that same passion as he always had for the lost of this world.

John's choice of college was Charleston Southern University (known then as Baptist College). We were scheduled for our furlough after Mission Meeting was over in late July, 1982.

We made arrangements with Elinor and Wayne Pennell to take care of Barney while we were on our furlough. Plans were for us to return to the Yogyakarta area for ministry, and it would be natural for Barney to adjust to the new home. He became a father while we were away. He and the Pennell's dog had two little puppies.

133

The Rutledge Avenue Baptist Church (now known as Rutledge Memorial) in Charleston was our host, providing a place for us to live while on furlough. This meant that our son could live with us while attending his first year of college. We enjoyed that furlough year immensely as the folks at Rutledge really shared their love and fellowship with us. We will always be grateful to this church and to Floyd and Shirley Whitfield for loving us as a family that year. This church performed a healing, loving ministry to us of which they are not fully aware.

From the outset of this furlough, Ray and I enlisted people to pray for us. While trying to live in the moment and enjoy each day as a family, in the back side of our minds was the idea of leaving John in the States while we returned to the other side of the world. We agonized in prayer together, and separately, as to God's will in the matter. We both felt a peace that we should return to carry out our call to take the gospel message. We talked together, prayed, and prepared for what was ahead of us. The year went by too fast!

Part 4

On the Move in Indonesia

On the Move in 1983

"God is our refuge and strength,
a very present help in trouble."
Psalm 46:1

We returned to Indonesia in August 1983. This time we were traveling without our son. John had completed one year in college and was ready to live in a dorm on campus for the first time. Plans were for him to room with a cousin, Stephen Hill, whom he was looking forward getting to know. After our departure, John would have one week before he could move to the dorm, so the folks at Rutledge Avenue Baptist Church allowed him to remain in the apartment until he could move to the campus.

This time our son would be on the other side of the world from us. Being a close family, our separation was like an unmanageable grief. We had done everything we could to prepare for this time, completely throwing ourselves on our Lord to hold us and sustain us.

In our conversation during those weeks prior to departure, I reminded John "to pray about everything." Praying aloud often brought greater comfort at times than praying silently, which I shared with him.

He added, "Yes, I know. I often prayed aloud during my high school years, and it helped me."

When we left the Charleston airport John was standing with Floyd and Shirley Whitfield. They planned to have breakfast together after our departure. We were both strong and did not break down as we said to our son, "We will count the months and days until June." Plans were made for him to return for a visit to Indonesia that following summer.

Our first rest stop was in Honolulu, where we stayed two full days and three nights. The grief of separation was heavy by then. We found ourselves down on our knees beside the bed in that hotel crying out for His strength and peace. We wept and prayed. Then came God's calming presence all over us. We felt his strength. God never fails His children. He gave us His assurance all would be well. He was in charge. Once again we surrendered our son to our Father, believing that "The one who calls you is faithful and He will do it" (I Thessalonians 5:24).

We were scheduled to make a move once we returned to Indonesia. For sixteen years, we had worked in Kediri, and we felt the Lord was leading us to another location. We were willing to go where no church had been established. The work in Kediri was well established and strong. This fact was an encouragement to us to move.

A Baptist Church in Yogyakarta made a request for a couple to work in the area of Wonosari, located in a mountain range 40 kilometers to the south of Yogya. No churches existed in this mountainous area. They made their request to our mission and to the national convention. A contact person had been identified as Pak Chris (a military man). He was willing for a Bible Study to be held in his home. He had nine children, and he wanted them to learn about the Bible. The chairman of our mission talked to us about this assignment. It was understood that we would move to this area upon the completion of our furlough.

There would be hardships since electricity was not reliable in this area. We were told to bring a generator back with us. A generator was donated by Calvary Baptist in Florence, SC. Water was difficult to find, as the area was rocky and difficult to drill. The mountains were mostly bare, due to the lack of moisture in this particular area. The land was filled with rocks, so we invested in well-drilling equipment. We felt all our bases were covered, and we were looking forward to opening this new work. Little did we know that a few surprises were waiting around the corner.

Upon our return, we moved our crated belongings that were stored in Kediri to Yogyakarta in Central Java. Moving from one area to another requires a lot of time and patience. We had to secure letters from the police, stating we had a good conduct standing; letters from immigration, officially moving us from one area to another; letters from the Religion Department, releasing our services from that area; and many more letters of various types.

Upon moving to Yogya, we had to immediately report ourselves to the police and present our letters from East Java. This process took three or four days. Everyone had to fill out a four-page form that included a brief life history, plus who our relatives are on both sides of the family, including aunts and uncles. We were finger-printed and had to present photocopies of all our credentials, along with several photos each. After completing the requirements at the police headquarters, we then proceeded to the immigration office where we went through a similar procedure of filling out forms, presenting photocopies of our credentials and filling out more forms. Their first request was to see our new police books, showing we were properly registered.

The next stop was the Religion Department. This department kept track of everyone connected to religions other than Islam. When we presented ourselves to the Department Head, he received us in a manner that seemed to be very warm. I immediately sensed something wasn't right in his demeanor but had no idea why. Then it became clear. He stated he had understood that Baptist were assigning another missionary to this area. He surprised us by saying, "I have written your national convention stating my objections."

We inquired, "May we ask why you are objecting?"

His objections to our being assigned to Yogyakarta were, "Two Baptist missionary couples are already here, and I can't approve your move to Wonosari because that area already has enough churches."

We knew that it was true, that there were two missionary units in Yogya, but each had different responsibilities in ministry. Elinor and Wayne Pennell were assigned to Seminary Extension, and Hazel and Tom Barron were assigned to student ministry. Also we emphasized we would not be living in Yogya but would move to the Wonosari area as soon as possible.

We were puzzled by his response, "Wonosari has enough Christians." One could count on both hands the number of Christians in that area, but to a Muslim, it was enough.

It was clear he had already made up his mind and would not allow another couple in Yogya, even with a clarification of duties.

Even though our assignment had been approved one year earlier, we became aware that the local national leaders had not approved our assignment. They made this known to the head of Religion Department in Yogya. Our own mission leadership had not been informed.

Even with that unsettling news, we, also, learned an independent Baptist group headed up by an Indonesian pastor had started work in the Wonosari area. They claimed that particular geographic area as theirs. This was known by the head of the Religion Department.

We were encouraged to find a place to live. The head of our national convention planned to appeal to the Religion Department in Yogya. For several weeks, we had been the guest of our friends the Pennells.

Ray and I found a house located within walking distance of the church we were working with in the Evangelistic outreach. The house was owned by an Indonesian surgeon who lived next door. It was fairly new with lots of very small rooms. We worked at making it comfortable, so it could feel like home. It had 1300 watts of electricity. This meant we had to unplug some appliances in order not to blow the fuse. We remained in Jogya for six months working with the local Baptist Church that was sponsoring the work. As often as possible, we went to the home of Pak Chris to teach.

In the meantime, our expiration date on our visa was fast approaching. We began the process to renew our visa. The religion head was a key person in the process of renewing our visa. We were able to get an extension of three months. That meant we could stay until January. If we did not have approval by January 7, 1984, we would have to leave the country.

Even though our status had been in limbo, we had continued faithful to the work God had put before us. In the back of our minds, we had faith that God would allow us to stay, so by this time we had established good relations with our sponsoring church and pastor. We were involved in much of their ministry and had started small groups that were meeting in homes. We were working in three different chapels and had started a Bible study on Tuesday evenings. Ray taught in the Seminary Extension program, and I was teaching the new Christians at our house, and teaching three women in the church how to read.

One of the ladies I was teaching how to read invited us to her home one night. She wanted to celebrate having electricity in her house by having some friends from the church. Her house had dirt floors and was about the size of a large dining room table. She had a total of 25 watts of electricity, and she was so happy! We all crowded in to give thanks and praise the Father for this blessing. The people were grateful for the smallest blessing and constantly reminded us we needed the spirit of praise and thanksgiving.

On several occasions over those months, I shared with Ray that I could envision the little town of Wonosari becoming a Christian village. It would be a place where everyone would worship the Lord. We would establish a church and the people of the community would know the joy of the Lord.

The folks prayed we would be permitted to continue to work with them. Approval for such an assignment would be necessary, and, as a practice, mission personnel were not assigned just to one church. Beside that reason, it was becoming evident that the head of the Religion Department in Yogya was not going to relent and allow us to stay. But we always stayed with something until it was completed, and we were finding it difficult to be pulled away.

Ray suggested we rise early while still dark and go in separate rooms to meditate on God's Word and pray. "Don't ask why" Ray said, "but let's spend our time listening and praising Him for our situation." We agreed!

This prayer was from some of my notes during this period:

Father, you have said that we should give thanks in all things. I want to give thanks for our circumstances. I want to thank you for allowing this situation to come in our lives. Lord, I don't understand what is happening but I do know that you are the same yesterday, today, and forever. I trust you, Father!

There were days when we would rather have curled up than stand up. Little by little, as we sought Him in those early morning hours, He was leading us on a spiritual journey of quiet reverence, reminding us that He is God. As Psalm 115:3 states, "Our God is in the heavens. He does whatever He pleases." We didn't need to understand the reasons why. He didn't need our advice or counsel. He only wanted our unreserved trust, love, and devotion.

A Baptist Church in Ambon needed help. One of our dedicated national leaders had been assigned to Ambon as an attorney for the government. He started the church and needed help to strengthen the believers. Also, there was work with a new group that had been started in another area of the island. This Indonesian leader approached us about taking this assignment for a few months until a new assignment could be determined. We agreed to go for two months. He requested that while we were in Ambon we pray about whether this was where the Lord wanted us to stay for this term of service.

During this time many of our mission colleagues came by to visit; some spent the night, but all prayed for us. They were our encouraging family, giving support when needed.

We packed and crated everything. Our belongings were stored in a warehouse in Yogya. Barney was turned over once again to the Pennells. We flew from the Yogya airport to Ambon.

Ambon, The Second Move

Ambon is another beautiful island in Indonesia. Located in the Maluku Islands, it is nestled in among the rolling hills that emptied into the ocean. At sunset when the lights of the city began to shine the same time as the sun set over the ocean, it was striking.

Ambon society had its beginnings as far back as the Portuguese, who established the fort of Kota Laha back in 1577. The Dutch eventually renamed it Fort Victoria. The Maluku's were known for spice trade. The *cengkek* (clove) is the number one crop in Ambon. The clove trees require little care. A mature tree yields anywhere from five to six kilograms of buds, which equals to 11 to 13 pounds. The Ambonese people make model boats, little houses, and other types of constructions entirely out of cloves. They discovered that sucking on a few whole cloves brings relief if they had a toothache.

Although part of Indonesia, Ambonese people understand and speak the Indonesian language, they have their own dialect and an entirely distinct culture. Ambon was a long distance from our mission base on Java. At this time we were wondering if we had missed God's intentions. We began to doubt if we were where He wanted us to be in the first place.

Over the next several months, reflecting and pondering what had happened, the Lord began to speak into our minds. God's ways are different. Because we couldn't carry out our assignment and live in the mountain village of Wonosari, did not mean we missed His purpose. In those six

145

months, we taught a lot of people and preached many sermons. We were used to bring three of the Pak Chris's children to the Lord and to strengthen their faith. We had precious time with our pastor and his wife in prayer and personal Bible study. Three Indonesian ladies in our sponsoring church learned how to read and write their names. We also had the privilege of giving support to Wayne and Elinor Pennell when their son, Mark, was killed in an accident while visiting them.

Ray and I have been blessed with a good relationship. It is good we enjoy being in each other's company. Ray always found something to laugh about or to joke about. It was a great joy to work together as a team, fulfilling our calling to take the gospel to the lost.

We were strengthened as a couple. We had always prayed together, but now our prayer times were like cold water to our souls. God united us as true partners in ministry and taught us to "Give thanks in every circumstance." We knew our enemy wanted us to give up. We were being tested. But our goal was to do the will of our Father, regardless of what we had to face. We knew He was with us. With this Ambon invitation, our prayer was for a new touch from the Holy Spirit for the ministry at hand.

God gave us Isaiah 41:9-10. "You are my servant, I have chosen you and have not rejected you. So do not fear, for I am with you; do not be dismayed, for I am your God. I will strengthen you and help you. I will uphold you with my righteous right hand."

A gentleman met us at the plane when we arrived on Ambon. He was an Indonesian version of Henry Kissinger (a former United States Secretary of State). He operated the restaurant inside the terminal and he was a member of the church. His hearty welcome and enthusiasm were an immediate encouragement to us. He took us to the city in his vehicle, sharing about the needs and the outreach ministry. Arrangements were made for us to stay at a hotel not far from the church.

We walked around the area, stopping to speak with people. A lovely lady came out to greet us in the road. She was very outgoing and friendly. We learned she was from Java and was married to an Ambonese. Upon learning where we were staying, she insisted we stay in her home. Our plans were to stay at the hotel until we could prepare a room in the back of the church building. She had a large house and took us inside to show us the room and bath. It was so much cleaner than the hotel. We agreed on cost and went immediately to get our things. In the yard of the house was a large banyon tree. The afternoon shade of that tree was an ideal place for people to meet with us. They were eager to hear the good news. We knew the Lord prepared this place for us. The lady provided fresh sheets every day; she prepared delicious food for us; she couldn't do enough; she became our family.

Our only news of the outside world came over a short wave radio. Telephone calls in those days were simply out of the question, because of poor connections. Letters took several weeks to arrive, even months. We were practically shut off from news from our son, other family members, and our mission family. If we had a major medical need, we had no help. Daily we laid ourselves on the Lord for all our needs.

One morning we were surprised by a visit from a New Tribes missionary. He and his family lived just outside the city. He rode a huge motorcycle. Being fellow Americans, he invited us to a hotdog dinner that evening. The wieners came from a can, but we were delighted!

During the meal, he shared they would be visiting their son in boarding school in another location in the country. They extended an invitation for us to stay in their home while they were away for that week. This would save some money and give us some time before moving to the room at the church.

Their rented house was located on a hill with lots of trees. They had a front porch the length of the house which we enjoyed in the afternoons. We would sit there reading or fellowshipping with those who stopped by. On the porch was a beautiful parrot with bright red, green, yellow plumage sitting on his perch.

One day men came to replace the floor tile on the porch, and a piece of tile became a flying missile. It hit the bird in the head and killed him. We marked the burial place so we could show the children where he was buried. We looked around at the bird market but could not find one just like theirs. We had ridden the motorcycle that was left for us to use when going to shop or to the church. While at the bird market, all the mirrors were stolen. The next day we spent time replacing the mirrors on the vehicle. We were happy to see them return without further mishaps.

Within two weeks, a room was completed for us at the church. They fixed a good-sized room into a small sitting area to greet folks, and the room behind was our bedroom.

The men made a frame, and we purchased a mattress to fit the frame. We had a one-eye kerosene stove on which to cook our food and boil our water. Screen wire was placed in the windows to keep out the mosquitoes. We used the restroom that was at the church. Four plastic chairs were placed in our sitting area to receive guests.

Oftentimes, we think we have to have certain things to function on a daily basis, but we discovered how little it takes to get by each day. We became great at one-pot meals. Fish was available and fresh every day at the local market. A heavy duty pot was found at the market that would fit nicely on our little kerosene burner. We learned what to cook first and then when to add it all together for our one-pot meals.

The church family was a real family to us. They were so proud to have us. There were endless opportunities to witness and to counsel. Many of the members in the church had some Christian background. The Maluku islands had been occupied by the Dutch and there were several large churches in the area that were built by the Dutch. Many thought they were Christians because their parents were called Christians. A large number of the members were not saved due to this misunderstanding.

On Sundays, Ray poured his heart out preaching the Word, and the Holy Spirit's anointing power was felt in our worship. In every service, someone would answer the invitation to accept Christ as their personal Lord and Savior. This brought a whole new attitude, a new atmosphere in the church. We were experiencing revival!

149

A Visit to our Outreach Ministry

A chapel had been started in an area that was difficult to reach. The journey required taking the ferry. A group would go on Sunday afternoons to this area. Several families came together in a home of one of the members to hear God's word taught.

Our second week in Ambon, we were informed it was time to make a trip to the outreach ministry. We left around 2:00 p.m. in a pickup truck. The flatbed was covered and benches reached all around the truck. Ray rode up front with the driver and a layman from the church. In the back with me were two women and two young men.

As we approached the area of the ferry, we stopped at a stop light. While waiting at the stop light, in hopped three young men in their late teens or early twenties. They didn't say anything as they pushed their way in among us. They were mumbling to themselves and snickering. They didn't notice that I was present until the truck started moving. Once they saw me, they enjoyed their muffled comments between them.

I noticed that our group was nervous. Being new, I didn't know they were gang members. I thought they were just rude young men imposing themselves on us for a ride. Upon arriving at the ferry, they got out of the truck to wait until we were on the ferry.

"What are we going to do?" exclaimed one of the women.

I inquired, "What do you mean?"

"Those young men are gang members and they will commandeer our vehicle," said the older woman in the group.

150

"How will they commandeer our vehicle?" I continued. "We will not allow that to happen!" I didn't know at that time what we would do, but I knew something had to be done!

"You don't understand! They probably have weapons. They will use them!" the older lady explained almost out of breath. She was afraid and so were the others.

I explained to Ray what was happening. He put the older woman up front in the cab and came back to sit with me and the others. While talking with the group, I learned that the church had rented the truck and driver to take the team out that Sunday afternoon. The church purchased the gas and paid for our ferry tickets. These three young men were imposing themselves on this group to pay for their tickets and risk further exploits once we arrived at our destination.

I decided that I would confront them with a question. "Did you purchase tickets for the ferry?"

They seemed startled but laughed. "No," they answered with an air of arrogance.

"Who paid for you?" I inquired.

"You did!" they answered, while snickering.

"Do you know who we are?" I asked, knowing that they didn't, but also knowing that it would be a way I could introduce our group.

"No, should we?" answered one of the men as if he could care less who we were!

"We are members of the local Baptist Church. We are going to a house where we will have a worship service. We will be there over an hour," I shared. "Where are you going?" I asked.

"We will ride around for a while," he replied.

I continued my conversation with them. "Since our church is paying for the use of this truck, for the gas, and for your ferry tickets, you will not use this truck while we are having our service. When we arrive at our destination, you will attend the service with us!"

Everyone in the group was really anxious by this time. Ray joined in and issued them an invitation to join us. He explained what we did in a worship service. They had the most startled look on their faces.

When we arrived, I said to them, "Come in with us!"

They got out of the truck and went inside the home with us. Everyone greeted them and made them feel welcomed. Everyone in our group kept looking at them and at each other. They could not believe what had happened.

A member gave them a song book. After listening for a few minutes, they joined in the singing. They were invited to introduce themselves, which they did. They listened intently to the message, prayers, and seem to enjoy the singing. They enjoyed the recognition they were given, and it was evident they enjoyed the refreshments and the fellowship.

On the way back to the city, they talked freely with our team members. They asked lots of questions about the scriptures, salvation, and the church. Feeling relieved, our members were entirely different people on the return trip.

Once we were back at our church, I shared that our evening service would begin in thirty minutes. I invited them to stay for worship. Two of the young men did stay, but one said he had to leave.

Our team rushed inside on arrival, sharing with the members that Ibu Joyce stood up to the gang members and they attended the service. After that experience, if the church had any type of problem that needed attention, they enjoyed suggesting, "Turn it over to Ibu Joyce! She can handle it!"

Thinking back over what happened, I was grateful that it turned out as well as it did. The group, along with Ray, commented that the three young men had an opportunity to hear the gospel, even though they had other intentions.

Day-to-Day Ministry

Ray taught seminary extension courses twice a week in the afternoon. They requested that I work with the youth. We started out with about ten young people and ended up with more than thirty. It was a real challenge to come up with interesting subjects, but the youth were responsive and enthusiastic. Every day members would bring by some friend or relative for us to explain how to be saved. These folks would also join in the worship on Sundays.

We would get cold, boxed-juice drinks from a nearby store, and in that store was a young man dressed like a girl, wearing lipstick, etc. We invited him to visit with us. He did, and we had opportunity to share God's love with him through scripture, testimony, and prayer. Before we left, he had returned to dressing like a young man.

Two months had passed when entering our room, we noticed that the screens at the windows had holes punched through them. After inquiring, one young man said that one of the younger boys did it so air could come into our room. They didn't have screens on their windows, and his concept was that it made the room hotter. We managed to tape paper over the holes, which lasted about a week.

Members would invite us to their homes and serve all the specialties from that area. One was *sago* dish. It was made from the *sago* tree, and the substance looked like white glue and was tasteless. The first time we tried it, the method of eating it was explained. You would hold the bowl up to your mouth and sup it up slowly. The art was not getting your nose in it. They wanted to watch us try it. I went first and passed their approval test. Ray looked down, and his nose touched the white sago paste. This delighted them! I am glad that we tried it, but once was enough.

After we had been there for about a month, the Baptist pastor located on a nearby island came to visit us. He invited us to come to Seram to his church and to go to the area that was being developed by the government to relocate people from the crowded island of Java. His church had a ministry among those who were relocated. We had been informed earlier that we would get an invitation to visit Seram and had been encouraged to go.

Two young men joined us on the trip. We took a ship from Ambon over to Seram. It took about two hours or more to reach the island. We spent the night in the home of the pastor, where a cot was offered to us. Everyone else found a place on the floor or sat up in a chair for the entire night.

Early the next morning, we rode on a truck to the dock where we would take a boat across the water to the other side. The waves were high, and it took about forty-five minutes to reach the shore. Once there, we boarded a truck and rode for about two hours to reach the new project where we stayed for one week. The pastor in charge prepared a place for us to stay with them. They had a simple little house with a well outside for their water. Catching the rain water in drums was another source of water when the well became dry during the dry season. They had some chickens and were raising rabbits to supplement their diet.

Everyday, we taught in their little church building with a dirt floor. They had planted flowers in their front yard and had looked for ways to make their place a home. Some of them walked for a couple of hours to be in church. They shared their hearts and lives with us. Everything they offered us was a sacrifice for them. There were no stores or medical facilities. We sat out in their yard and looked at the stars and listened to the many sounds coming from the jungle.

The pastor wanted to prepare a chicken for our going-away meal. He proceeded to place a small rope like a lasso on the ground for the chosen chicken to step into. Once the chicken stepped into the lasso, he drew the rope around its leg. After placing corn around the place where the rope was, he waited for the chicken to step in the loop. He waited and waited. Having grown up on a farm, I had to resist reaching down and picking the chicken up with my hands. I convinced myself I would wait for his method to work because I could not afford as his guest to cause him embarrassment. Time came for us to leave for the church and still no chicken. We had dried fish again along with our rice.

Several of the folks accompanied us to the seaside where we took the boat across to the other side. In order to get to the seaside to take the boat, we had to cross over a river. We received word the bridge was out, so we had to go into the river to get to the other side where the truck was waiting. The pastor and a layman helped me get through the rushing water. We climbed into the back of the truck and most of us were dry by the time we arrived at the seaside.

The pastor's wife was terrified of the water since she didn't know how to swim. We sat face-to-face in the boat, and I held her hands as the waves lapped into the boat. One person was constantly bailing water.

"Look up, not down!" I suggested.

I prayed her through the brief journey. That evening we all had worship with the folks at the church on Seram.

Early the next morning we set out to the dock where the ship would come to take us back to Ambon. Saying farewell to the pastor's wife I whispered, "Don't be afraid returning in the boat. I can't swim either!"

A huge smile crossed her face. "Really! If you aren't afraid and can't swim then I won't be afraid," she shared as if she had new insight.

They all got up while still dark and traveled by truck to the dock. They stood on the dock and waved until we were out of sight. We often laugh, saying that we have been beyond the "Great Commission." This place had to be at least ten miles beyond! God has his people everywhere. What a joy for us to go to them!

Two weeks after returning from Seram, our church had a day together on the beach. Everyone brought food to share. We held worship service on the shore, and Ray baptized thirteen people. They lined up in the water, waiting for their turn to be baptized in the ocean. It was a beautiful day in the Lord.

Our promise to stay two months extended into three months. Word came that the convention leadership and mission leaders had approved an invitation for us to either work in a small city near Kediri or remain in Ambon. We had heard earlier that a national pastor may be considered for the Ambon ministry. Once again we had a group of believers asking us to remain with them. We spent time in prayer as it was a difficult decision to make. Almost everyone cried, including us. We felt if they could secure a national pastor that it would be best for the work. We considered the ministry back on Java.

It was time for us to return to Jakarta, the capital city, to give a report concerning the work. The Kebayaran Baptist Church was the sponsoring church for the work in Ambon, so Ray was invited to bring the Sunday morning message, reporting on the work we did while in Ambon. This time would coincide with John's arrival from the States. We were in Jakarta when John and some other MK's arrived together. It was a great reunion!

Summer Together in Surabaya

We spent June to August in Surabaya, the second largest city in Indonesia. An available mission house was offered to us to use until we could move to Mojokerta, our next place of service. Charles and Barbara Cole lived in the house in front of us. They were very helpful. It was a good place to be while John was visiting us.

One day, John was invited to swim at the Hyatt Hotel by a friend of ours. He became over-heated and that, coupled with something he ate, caused him to pass out. He hit his head while falling, which called for stitches. Once again God provided! One of our nurses was in town for the day, and she was getting ready to leave the city. She ministered to John. He would need to go to the hospital, and she insisted we go with her to Kediri. Ray stayed behind due to engagements and guests that were coming. He would join us later. John stayed in the hospital overnight. We were able to get some rest in Kediri, which was like home to us.

Our area director, Dr. Bill Wakefield, and his wife, Delcie, were coming for a visit to Surabaya and then on to Kediri. Ray had the opportunity to sit down with them in Surabaya and share about our experiences since returning from furlough. Ray shared with me later that it was a healing experience for him to open and share his heart with these two servants. While in Kediri, I had the opportunity to share with them, also. We will always remember the compassion and the understanding they showed to us and the prayer time that we shared together.

159

It had been almost a year since having a place to settle. We had been moving from one ministry to another. Time back together as a family gave us an opportunity to talk, to share, to heal. Once again, God was faithful to provide all that we needed.

John returned to the States to begin his junior year in college, and we made preparations to move to our next place of service. While preparing our rented house for occupancy, Ray became very ill. He had high fever and was nauseated. He took some medicine that we had for fever and felt better. The next week he came down with chills and fever, so we took him to our Baptist Hospital in Kediri. He was in the hospital for over one week, having tests made. He was very ill. The medical missionaries thought he had tuberculosis of the kidneys. They suggested Ray be sent to Singapore to a urologist. The night before we left for Singapore, four laymen from Setia Bakti (Faithful) Baptist Church in Kediri came to pray for him. They put oil on his forehead and laid their hands on him when they prayed. He noticed immediately that he felt better and was able to sit up.

We left the next morning, armed with all his x-rays to see the urologist in Singapore. Upon arrival, we went immediately to the doctor's office and presented the x-rays. He said that it did look like tuberculosis of the kidney, but he would make his own x-rays and run some tests.

After several days, we returned to his office to hear the results of the tests. He put up the x-rays we brought with us, and then put up beside them the new ones he had made. He said to us, "This is the kidney that has the disease, and over here is the same kidney, but it looks brand new. "Mr. Rogers, what do you think could have happened?"

"The evening before I left Kediri, four men from my former church came to pray for me. They anointed my forehead with oil and asked the Lord for healing." Ray shared with the doctor. "I felt better immediately!"

"Mr. Rogers, their prayers worked! You do not need any medicine. You are well!"

God is faithful! It was just another reason to rejoice!

Mojokerto, The Third Move
1984 – 1988

Mojokerto is a small city of approximately one million people. A house was found within walking distance to the only Baptist Church. The house was in great need of repair. We put screens on the windows and doors, and repaired the bathrooms. After several weeks of repairing and painting, it was finally livable and we prepared to move.

We began a work located about three miles from the church at the opposite end of the city. Bapak Matadji, a member of the local Baptist church, offered his home for the ministry. Bapak Matadji was a school teacher. He and his wife, Ibu Matadji, had six children. It was a wonderful surprise to find Ibu Matadji had been a young person in my Sunday school class when we lived in Solo. When she approached me she said, "Ibu Rogers, do you remember me?" She and Matadji met at the Baptist Seminary during a young people's conference. Once she refreshed my memory, I did remember her. The oldest of their children was Daniel. He was sixteen at the time. They had saved money for his education, and Daniel had excelled academically. It was their desire that he go to the university in Surabaya.

Around the middle of October, the young people were practicing for a Christmas play at their home. Ibu had made tea for everyone She was bringing a tray from the back of her house on the outside, so as not to disturb the practice session in their sitting room. She slipped and fell by the well and could not get up by herself. Many came to assist her and brought her back inside, and she was placed on her bed. We offered to take her in our car to the doctor. She insisted that she would be fine and would wait until morning to decide whether she would see a doctor. When we arrived the next morning, her right leg was badly swollen. We offered to take her to Kediri to our Baptist Hospital, which was about an hour's drive. Daniel went with us.

When Dr. Don Duvall examined her and made x-rays, he called us in to see the results. Cancer was throughout her body, and that was what had caused the break. He explained that he would not be able to operate under those conditions. He wanted to know if he should tell her, or if we should be the ones. We encouraged him to tell her. We were in the room when he shared the news. We knew that she was strong in her faith and would be able to hear this sad news, which she did. They determined that it would not be wise to have surgery. She was to rest and use crutches. We wanted her to allow us to bring Daniel in so he could understand. She did not want her son to know her condition. She insisted we not tell him or any member of her family. This she would do once she found the proper time. We encouraged her not to delay telling them.

Her husband kept inquiring about why they did not help her with the broken bone in the upper right leg. It was almost two months later, and she still had not shared the news about her condition. They could see she was getting thinner and was weakening. We finally had to share with him her true condition. So little could be done for her. The group had been praying; but once they were informed to her true condition, a prayer chain was formed to pray for her. This was around Christmas time.

I spent some days with her while her family was at school. She was always happy to see me, and she suffered without complaining. Tumors were growing throughout her body, and one was getting rather large on her forehead. She went to be with our Father and became free of pain on March 10 at 7:30 a.m. in 1985. She was 40 years old. A large number of church members had spent the night. They went back to their homes at 5:30 a.m. We arrived at 7:00 a.m. that day when she took her last breath. Only we and the immediate family were present. Thirty minutes later her Moslem neighbors began to arrive. They made themselves available to assist in any way they could. When I realized they were looking to me to take charge, I knew then that the Lord was giving me an opened door to witness. It was my prayer I would not waste this great opportunity.

While living in Kediri, an opportunity to learn how to prepare a body for burial had been offered to the women of my church. I felt it was for the nationals, and I really felt out of place. The Holy Spirit kept nudging me to attend, even though I felt I would never have to use the information. I was the only missionary who attended. Six years had passed, and now I understood why the Holy Spirit wanted me to attend this conference on "How to prepare the dead for burial."

Once we were organized and everyone knew what to do, we began the process of preparing the body of our friend and neighbor. While we were bathing her body, first in soapy water and the second time in tea to give color, I realized I had a captive audience, and everyone in the room was a Moslem. I began to share with them about what happens when a Christian dies. I explained Ibu Matadji was with the

Lord. The body we were preparing for burial would decay; but her soul lived, and she was in the presence of the Lord. She was with the Lord because she had accepted Christ Jesus as her Savior and Lord. They too could have that same assurance once they believed in Christ Jesus. They were very appreciative of my explanation and thanked me for sharing. They were very attentive to everything I said.

The casket was lined with sateen material, and we put little live pink roses all over the material. Underneath the sateen we placed fragrant leaves. She was dressed and white ginger flowers were placed in her hair. Burial takes place within the same day the person dies, so she was buried by 2:00 p.m. that afternoon. The service was held at the home with hundreds in attendance. Then the body was taken to the gravesite.

Our group continued to meet in Matadji's home. This was an encouragement to them. Little by little, the family adjusted to life without their mother. That following September, Daniel entered the university in Surabaya.

Eli was an eight- year- old boy in our group. His parents were neighbors of Matadji, and they were faithful in attendance. Eli had an open drainage from his brain that caused a large growth on the side of his nose. This growth grew larger and was closing his right eye. He was afraid to go out in public and tried to hide behind his mother. He did feel comfortable to come to Sunday school and to worship. If something was not done for Eli, his condition would cause his death.

With the help of a friend in Surabaya we were able to meet a neurosurgeon. He agreed to examine Eli and determine whether or not he could help him. Arrangements were made to take him to Surabaya to have the examination. The doctor said that he would be able to perform the surgery, and he would not charge his regular fee. Eli's surgery was successful, and several helped to contribute to that success, including Dr. Ken Hinton from our hospital in Kediri. It was a marvelous change in that little fellow. He was happy and demonstrated a new level of confidence.

The Lord blessed our outreach ministry. In all, five groups were established. Everyday, we met with a different group for Bible study.

Our telephone service was much better at this time than earlier days. We were able to make calls and receive them without too much difficulty. It was August, 1985, when John called.

We were excited to hear from him. "What is it like to be the President of the Student body?" Ray inquired. "Are you enjoying your classes? Do you like your teachers?" We bombarded him with questions about school, etc. We finally sensed that something wasn't right, and we asked, "Is anything wrong?"

He was hesitant, "Dad... I'm sorry, but I have some bad news... your mom died!"

Ray was not able to return for the funeral. John drove from Charleston to Wilmington, N.C. to represent our family. Grieving without a funeral or a gathering with others is an experience in itself. Ray had now lost both his parents while away. Picturing our loved ones in heaven with the Lord helped take away the sorrow.

Our helper from Kediri moved to Mojokerto to live in our home and to work for us. After a brief period of time, her husband joined her and did our yard work. He was not in good health but was helpful in many ways.

Ray invited him to sit with him in our living room where a chalk board was on the wall. Ray used that board to illustrate the gospel to those who visited or came for Bible study. On it, Ray had drawn a picture of a ship on the sea. People were in the water with arms raised calling out for help. Life preservers were thrown out to the people to be saved. Ray explained to Pak Dul the gospel using the illustration on the board.

Pak Dul leaned forward in his chair as if he did not want to miss any part of the story. He said, "I'm like the ones in the water calling for help."

Pak Dul prayed to accept Christ as Savior and Lord. Our helper, Ibu Uyu had accepted Christ several years earlier.

Shifting Politics

Christianity was growing fast and the government was becoming concerned. One way to curtail growth was to limit the number of missionaries, so for several years we had heard that the Indonesian government was not renewing visas for some missionaries from other groups. Our Baptist missionaries had not been rejected on visa renewals, but we knew that our time would likely come. Our mission made preparation for the inevitable. The Indonesian government then made a decision to limit the number of years the missionary could remain in their country. Any one who had been in their country longer than ten years would have to leave, which meant the majority of us. Our visa was denied in November 1988, along with fifty-two others.

Invitations to work in Australia, Philippines, or New Zealand were placed on the table for us to consider and pray about once we left Indonesia. The right choice for us, as directed by the Holy Spirit, was New Zealand. The opportunity in Australia would not have allowed us to establish an indigenous church, as the church would remain under the care of the mother church. In New Zealand we had the freedom to establish a church that would be indigenous. We were to work with the New Zealand Baptist Union in planting a church in the Manurea area of Auckland. The assignment was for two years.

Thinking about leaving the country I wanted another opportunity to visit with the missionaries and our national friends in Kediri. Ray was very busy and couldn't leave the work. "Would you mind if I took the bus?' I asked Ray. Kediri is one hour away by car and a little longer by bus.

"That is a good idea!" he responded.

To my great surprise, when I boarded the bus, there were many empty seats! I was able to ride with only one other person seated beside me. We made a stop at a small town before we took the Kediri road, and one more person joined us on our seat. I was seated on the aisle, and after we started moving again, the young man who sat on the seat with me and another woman, moved beside me. He immediately wanted to know where I was going, where I came from, where I lived, why was I going to Kediri, and on and on.

He finally got to the question that most people asked and that was, "Why are you in Indonesia?"

This always opened the door to share my testimony. He was intrigued. He interrupted by saying, "I attended a Christmas program once with a Christian friend!"

Upon inquiring, "What do you know about Jesus?" he could not answer.

"I think he was a good prophet" he finally said.

I had made it a practice to carry with me tracts, a pencil, note paper, so I could share the difference between religion and a relationship with Christ by using the bridge as shown in the "Four Spiritual Laws" tract. I went through the whole process of drawing the bridge and showing how man was separated from God by sin and that Christ's dying on the cross bridged the gap between God and man.

Up to this point, he had been saying that we would all end up in heaven. "We only have different ways to get there, but all ways will lead us to heaven!" When he saw this bridge, and it was clear that only through Christ would we be saved, he had something new to consider.

About that time, the conductor called out his place of departure. He got up to leave and stood for a moment looking at me speaking in the Indonesian language so those around could hear, "You are telling me that there is only *one* way to Allah (God) and that is through Jesus Christ!"

"Yes!" that is correct.

"I have never heard this before. I will not forget this day!" he turned and left the bus.

I never saw him again, but I often think about him and pray that he has found Christ as his Savior.

Once again we began to make preparation to leave the country. We gave away most of our things, sold others, and packed up what we wanted to take with us to New Zealand. We found a perfect, loving home for Barney, knowing that we could not take him with us.

Again, saying good-bye is never a simple thing in Indonesia. It takes days and weeks. Many farewells were held to wish us a safe journey. The most meaningful of all to me was a farewell that was not known or planned. When we left Pak Matadji's home, the ladies who had worked with me to prepare Ibu Matadji's body for burial had come out of their homes and lined the small roadway on each side to wave good-bye to us. We have prayed many times that those seeds that were planted that day of the burial would bear fruit for His glory.

Several weeks later, we flew out of Jakarta for the final time as missionaries to Indonesia. We had given twenty-six years to the people and had been privileged to serve in His name. I recall looking out of the window of the plane as we turned to leave the country. We plowed hard ground in places; fought rocks, weeds, and thistles; planted seeds in fertile ground; and saw harvest come forth. We had reaped the joy of the harvest, and now another door was opening in a different land. The people of Indonesia would always have a special place in our hearts. We rejoiced that we were able to live and work among them for those twenty-six years. We rejoiced that many have their names written in heaven, and we would see them again.

Part 5

A New Country

The Land of the Long, White Cloud

"All the ends of the earth will remember and turn to the Lord, and all the families of the nations will worship before you. For the kingdom is the Lord's and He rules over the nations." Psalm 22:27-28

New Zealand is an island nation, remote, set apart, in a corner of the world's largest ocean. It is often referred to as the "Land of the Long, White Cloud"

Looking out the window of our plane as we approached for landing, thousands of yachts and sailboats speckled the sea. We saw the lush greenery and the beautiful shore line that serves as a natural "boundary" for the North and South Islands that make up the nation of New Zealand.

Before we were allowed to leave the plane, a group came on to spray the inside of the plane. We were told not to worry, that the spray would not harm us. They did this to protect their small island country from disease and affliction that might be brought in by passengers and their luggage.

After clearing immigration and getting our luggage, we headed out the arrival corridor. A large banner with, "Welcome! Ray and Joyce," could be seen from a distance. Around twenty individuals came to greet us.

One of the attractions to the New Zealand assignment was not having to learn a new language. The first thing we noticed, though, was their style and expression in speaking English. They also made immediate comment about my southern accent. We learned many expressions and meanings during our time there. For instance, to be invited to *tea* is really dinner. *A cupa* is a cup of tea. They often use the word *shout* to mean a treat for them. You can *shout* someone a trip, a meal, or even a cupa.

They took us to the home of Ray and Doreen Stirling. They had been long-time members of the Manurea Baptist Church and wanted to be a part of the new church we were establishing. They were in their early sixties. We visited with everyone and had some biscuits (cookies) and a cupa.

Bob and Beth Weaver, members, were in the USA for one month. Bob was sent by his company for training. They had offered us their home while they were away. Their house was on a cul de sac and was conveniently located near a supermarket. We settled in and began our work.

A member of the Manurea Baptist Church visited us and gave us the name of a Maori woman who had recently moved in the community. We took her name and address and went immediately to visit her. When we arrived, we called out for her at the gate of her yard. She came out and we greeted each other, and she promised us immediately that she would go with us to church on Sunday. This was our first service at the church, and we brought Alice with us. She became a strong faithful member and a wonderful prayer partner.

Ten members from the sponsoring Manurea Baptist Church joined together with us to begin a new church in the Clendon Park Community. These members had already started meeting in the local Clendon Park Community Center. The group had reached around thirty when they began to worship each week. A Sunday School for the smaller kids had been started. Two of the ladies were teaching during the worship hour. The adults and young people met in a home during the week for Bible Study.

The New Zealand Baptist Union requested us to serve for two years. This was a fraternal relationship with our Board and their Union. Our support would still come from the International Mission Board. One other couple, Rick and Beth Wolfe, were assigned to New Zealand and had been in the country over a year when we arrived. They were located about four hours drive from us and had two children, a boy and a girl. New Zealand was their first assignment. They were able to help this senior couple with needed information and encouragement.

A committee from the church was in charge of finding us a house to rent. One was located just within walking distance of the Community Center.

We spent hours making contacts through visitation in homes, talking with people in the shops, and following up on those who visited on Sundays. Our congregation was diverse, representing many groups. The Church looked like our community. There were Samoans, Maoris, Fijians, and the European Kiwi's. In a year, the group grew to over sixty in attendance and about thirty children in Sunday School. A large number in the community were single-parent homes. They were also on the *dole* (welfare). We found that some would live together rather than marry so they could claim two welfare checks instead of one. Most of the families had dogs. They were Dobermans, Rottweillers, and other types of attack dogs. Most of them were well trained. The owners would call out, "He won't hurt you!" With that reassurance, I would cautiously move forward.

Everyone in our fellowship had their dog story. One Saturday afternoon, several of us were visiting in a community together. I found the house I was looking for, while others made contact at other homes. The front door was wide open, and I called out several times. No one came. I thought they may be outside in their backyard. As I started to move from the front, a large Doberman was watching me. He stood and got in position to attack. We had already prayed that the Lord would protect us as we visited, and as we went into each house we would be praying. I knew if I moved, he would leap toward me. I silently called out to the Lord for help. I found myself saying, "In the name of Jesus, sit!"

This dog sat down! I backed down the steps, not turning away from him. I found my way out of that yard. As I looked back, the dog was still sitting. What a wonderful Lord!

Once Ray was accompanied out of a yard by a German shepherd. He took Ray's shirt sleeve in his mouth and escorted Ray out of the yard to the sidewalk and then went back to his yard.

Nine out of ten in our little community did not go to church. They simply did not have a desire to know God. Their hearts were hard. One day I approached a man in his yard working on his car. He said that he was the only person home. My friend who was with me stood near the car. I shared with him about our church fellowship and invited him to come.

He replied, "I don't believe there is a God and if there is...he has never done anything for me!"

His comments touched me and tears came down my checks.

He looked at me and said, "I hope you aren't crying for me. No one has ever shed a tear for me before!"

I told him that it broke my heart because he did not know all that he was missing. Then I shared what Jesus meant to me. I could see that he was visibly moved but still had that hard heart. I told him I would return another time with my husband, and we would share more with him.

He thanked me, but I never saw him again. He moved the following week. I still pray for him that the seeds that were planted that day will bring forth fruit.

As a church, we were all praying about securing property for the future church building. The land we desired for the future church was fast being purchased, so we knew that it was time to find the property the Lord had for us.

A committee was formed to look for property. In the meantime, several members joined together to have garage sales to raise money for the purchase. All the original members tithed. The offerings grew. As we had very little expense, most of it was saved for the purchase of property.

The perfect location was found. It was on a hill that overlooked the shopping center at Clendon. They were able to purchase two sections, side-by-side. An architect was employed to draw up the plans for the church building on that particular property. They had worked so hard that we were able to purchase the property without going into debt!

Ray challenged them to begin saving for the building. They agreed that they would take up the challenge to build. Whatever they were called on to do, they did it! We had formed a real bond with the folks. They seem to be very reserved at first until they got to know and trust a person. Once they trusted us, then we were friends for life.

During this time, I had an opportunity, along with the associate pastor's wife at the sponsoring church, to take a course in financial planning. Most all of our neighbors, and those in our community, needed help budgeting their money. Many would spend their money and still have unpaid bills and no funds for food. I took the two-month course that trained volunteers how to budget a family's income.

It was a difficult course with lots of homework. We started out with over forty people in the class and ended up with only fourteen finishing. On the day of graduation, the head of the welfare department said that I was the only American who had ever taken the course. I received a certificate and was given a desk in the Welfare office near where I lived. I volunteered once a week for six hours. I had several clients and enjoyed my contact with them. I was able to witness to them, and pray for them. Some responded by visiting our church on Sundays. This was a valuable contact with the community and a service that I could give to the people. Many were helped, but there were some who struggled with learning discipline in budgeting their funds.

I requested one lady take the money that was allocated for her light bill and pay the bill immediately. She was instructed to return once the bill was paid. She came back in an hour having taken the money to buy herself a pair of shoes. The light bill still wasn't paid. As she took the new shoes out of her bag to show to me, I could feel my frustration reaching its limits.

"Why did you buy new shoes when you know your lights will be turned off shortly?"

She had a sheepish look, "They were so pretty!"

I remember telling her that she could enjoy looking at them in the dark when her lights were turned off. I told her to put them back in the bag and ask to see the receipt. I took her back to the shoe store, and she got her money back, and we went to the light company and paid her bill.

Once that was done, I said to her, "Do you want my help or not?"

"Yes, I do! I won't do this again," she said.

It took a lot of work with this woman, but she finally caught on and was doing well when I had to leave.

Ray/Joyce in the Lord

Unexpected blessings come from the mouths of children at times. The women would volunteer to work with the children in Sunday school so the same person wouldn't have to miss the worship hour every Sunday. I was volunteering one Sunday when the children were given an opportunity to suggest songs for the children to sing. In this group was a seven year old Chinese boy. His family came from Singapore and his father was working as a chef in one of the Chinese restaurants in Auckland. They came from a Buddhist background, and the boy was not familiar with the songs that we would sing in Sunday school and church. He suggested that we sing, "that song about our pastor and his wife."

The children and I looked at one another completely perplexed.

He continued, "You know that song that says, 'Ray/Joyce in the Lord always, and again I say Ray/Joyce.'"

We all laughed and sang, "Rejoice in the Lord always, and again I say rejoice."

I couldn't wait to tell Ray about what happened! Sharing this with him, he commented, "That child blessed us without even knowing it! What a great way for people to remember our names!" he said.

"And it serves as a reminder that we should 'rejoice in the Lord always' as the scripture says," I added.

Time to Move On

The chairman of evangelism and church growth requested that we stay and take another assignment remaining in New Zealand for another two years. He was told by our Area Director, Jerry Rankin, that we would need a job description before he would agree for us to remain.

This man had a heart for missions, and he had a vision to see churches planted throughout the Auckland area. He did *not* have the support from others to join him in that vision. We remained on scheduled to leave. An invitation had already been issued for us to join the first itinerant mission team formed in South and Central Asia.

A young man who had graduated from the church growth school was a prospect to become their next pastor. The land was purchased and debt free, and they had raised $60,000 toward the building. God had blessed!

A Return Trip

Two years later we received an invitation to return for the dedication of the first unit of the new building. We were given permission to go to New Zealand upon the completion of our furlough for the dedication.

The Lord had a surprise for us when we returned to the church. A new member said to us, "You think you have returned to New Zealand for the dedication of the building, but you really have returned so I would have an opportunity to apologize to you!"

When we had lived in this community before, this man was living with a woman but not married to her. At the time, the woman had a lovely daughter by her first marriage. Rachel was a seven year old attending our Sunday school. She was picked up each Sunday by Bob and Beth Weaver and brought to church. We went on several occasions to visit with Rachel and her mother in her home. Rachel's mom would welcome us, and each time we had a meaningful visit. We encouraged her to come with Rachel. Our visits would be concluded by having prayer for them, which they welcomed. However, whenever this man was home, he would be disrespectful and would not allow us to enter the home. He even asked us to leave. "I don't have time for you. And don't bother to return!" he would yell out to us.

Three days before we were to depart from New Zealand, he called saying they wanted to get married. A baby was on the way, and they wanted to be married as soon as possible. Ray told them that he did not have the time to perform their marriage ceremony for them as he would require that they come for counseling first, and we were due to leave the country shortly. He put them in touch with the associate pastor of Manurea Baptist Church. This pastor brought both of them to the Lord in the course of counseling.

After he became a Christian, this man had become convicted by the way he had treated others. He often wished that he could speak with us. He deeply regretted his actions and attitude toward us. When he heard that we would be returning he said, "I knew the Lord was giving me this opportunity to speak in person and asked your forgiveness." He had committed to memory many verses of scripture and shared that he felt the Lord was calling him to preach.

Jesus is the answer for all of man's needs. He takes the worst of us and makes us useful servants. It was a joyful experience. Christ always makes a difference in one's life. We thought we were returning to dedicate the new addition of the building, but our wonderful Lord had another blessing in store for us. Just another reason to rejoice!

❧

Part 6

Living out of a Suitcase

❧

Pakistan

China

• Chandigarh

Nepal

• Delhi

• Agra

India

• Calcutta

• Bhubaneshwar

Mumbai
(Bombay)

Secunderabad

• Hyderabad

Vishaktapatnam

Chennai

BANgalore

Indian Ocean

Bay of Bengal

Southern Asia Pacific Mission Team
1991 - 1997

"God who began the good work within you will keep right on helping you grow in His grace until His work within you is finally finished on that day when Jesus returns."
Phil. 1:6

Southern Asia Pacific Mission (SAPIM), later renamed Leadership, Evangelism, and Discipleship (LEAD), was the name for the itinerant mission team. This group was formed in 1988.

The team came into existence when many of us left Indonesia because our visas were not renewed. Our strategy was to minister to Christians in countries which did not grant full-time missionaries long-term visas. We did this by using the visitor's visa. Our ministry was providing teaching, training, and discipling to pastors, laymen, and women in order that they could in turn do the same for their people whom they served. The team's motto was 2 Timothy 2:2, "And the things you have heard me say in the presence of many witnesses entrust to reliable men who will teach others."

Courses were written by team members and translated into various languages. When we taught the course using the English language, most always we had a translator to stand by us. Even though many of the pastors and laymen understood English we did not want them to be confused and not get the true meaning of what we were teaching. When they left our seminars, they had a copy of the book

189

that was taught in their own language to take home to entrust to their people.

Three couples among our colleagues from Indonesia formed the original team. They were Clyde and Elaine Meador, Jim and Carolyn McAtee, and Von and Marge Worten. This was the year that Ray and I left for New Zealand. When we joined the team, another couple who had served in Malaysia and Fiji, Hugh and Katherine Smith, made up the team of five couples.

The place where we started out in 1963 was now again home for us during our itinerant ministry. We had an apartment as our base from which we could come and go to other places was in Penang. When we were not there, the apartment served as a guest house for missionaries who came to visit their children who were in high school.

We were blessed with wonderful neighbors. Tom and Sunny and their grown daughter, Jean, were our next door neighbors. They were a blessing from the outset. They were committed Christians and became prayer warriors for us and our ministry.

Our first Sunday back in Penang, we made our way to the Georgetown Baptist Church. As we walked into the parking lot of the church, we were immediately recognized by Sybil, whom we knew as a teenager. After all those years, she knew who we were! It was a joyful reunion. She immediately called her brother, Danny, and her older sister. We were thrilled to see many of the members again.

In the service that day was Dr. Oh Lock Hing and Dr. Oh Lock Ming. They welcomed us with great joy. We rejoiced together as we shared with them that Penang would be our base, and we would be able to see them more often in our final years of ministry.

The itinerant team members were not assigned a vehicle, but at times we did have access to a car when we were in Penang. We used public transportation wherever we were. The missionaries were thoughtful and did offer to pick us up for meetings and get-togethers. The church was a good distance from our apartment. Some of our longtime friends introduced us to some families located in our area who were members at the church.

One young couple, Kin Choy and Mary, lived nearby our apartment. They said they would pick us up for church when we were in town. They also held the weekly cell group in their home, and we became a part of this group.

Ray and I spent a total of seven years with the team, traveling to many countries. Over the period of those seven years, this Penang group of young married couples and some singles became family to us. They kept a copy of our itinerary and prayed for us daily when we were in other countries. They welcomed us back each time and gave us the opportunity to share what had gone on during our journeys to various places. God blessed us richly with the support and love from this group and from our neighbors. Each time we returned to our base in Penang, our loving neighbors would come welcoming us, embracing us, and bringing food items. They gave us their love, prayers, and encouragement.

I will always be grateful that we were in Penang when our son, John, called sharing that Mom had gone to be with the Lord. She was one month away from being ninety-four. She had suffered greatly with crippling arthritis and her hands were curled inward. Not having the opportunity to return for the funeral, our cell group, church friends, and neighbors gave their loving support through prayers and kindness. God is good! God never fails His children. We rejoice each time these dear people come to our minds and hearts.

Meanwhile, the work with the itinerant mission team allowed us to minister to many people, some of whom I will share in this section of the book because they are well known. Other names and/or stories I cannot share because of past and present political conditions.

India

We spent at least four months out of each year in India, so I will begin by sharing some experiences we had in that great land. Neither Ray nor I had ever had a desire to go to India prior to joining the team. We had landed down in Calcutta on one occasion in our travels, but had not ever visited the country. It proved to be a huge surprise to us!

India is the world's second most populous country, boasting a population of 1.1 billion. It is the world's largest democratic republic. Nearly two-thirds of their population depend on agriculture for their livelihood. Hindi is their national language.

Wherever you go in India, the country is vibrantly alive. India wrapped itself around us and drew us to its people, culture, food, and country. There is an energy about the people that is unequal anywhere else. Each region of India has its own language, music, dance, painting, food, architecture, and dress. In India, we met some of the most creative, intelligent, and dedicated people we have ever encountered.

Our ministry took us to the snow-capped mountains of the northern range near Nepal, from Delhi to Mumbai (Bombay), to Chandigarh, to the stupendous forts and palaces of Hyderabad and twin city of Secunderbad, to the tropical beaches of Madras, and to the bustling city of Bangalore.

Traveling in India

There were many interesting happenings while we traveled in the country. Traveling by train always promised an adventure. The train stations were brimming over with people, baggage, boxes of produce, dry goods, cargo of various kinds, etc. that we weaved in and out among to get to the train.

It was always confusing whether to board from the back of the train car or the front to reach our seats. If we boarded at the back and our seats were at the other end, then it was almost impossible to get to our seats. The train would often be moving before passengers could get to their seats because of having to pass over people in the aisle coming from the opposite end. The overhead space would be claimed by others if we were late getting to our seat, and then our luggage had to go where we could not look after it. It was important to have our luggage close by to make sure it was safe. We were fortunate more times than not getting to the right seat and having space overhead.

On one of the many trips we took, a middle age man sat directly across from us. He had one medium sized suitcase. When evening came he opened up his suitcase and took out a chain and a lock. We watched as he proceeded to chain the suitcase to himself and padlock it to his ankle. He slept soundly throughout the night. When he started to snore, we were tempted to pull on the chain that was locked to his ankle, but we didn't.

It was the usual course of things to sit on the tracks for hours at certain points along the way to wait on an oncoming train to pass by before we could proceed. If the train was late, it only added to the waiting time. Some passengers would get off the train and stand by the tracks to get some fresh air or walk around to pass the time, especially if it was day time.

It was not unusual on some trains for animals and chickens to travel right along with the passengers. They were being taken to sell or to give as a gift to those they would be visiting. It surprised us all at daybreak on one trip when a rooster started crowing from under the seat. That was a wake-up call for those who might have been asleep.

A few passengers actually had their one-eye kerosene stove with them to cook their rice or to boil water for their tea. This was a dangerous practice and wasn't permitted, but there were those who tried to get away with it and did.

Traveling by plane was always a reminder to us of how our Heavenly Father was looking after us. Safety pre-cautions were in place in many countries long before the USA started screening with any seriousness. Women and men passed through a closet-type booth where screeners were waiting to screen each individual. Women assisted women and men assisted the men. Once the luggage was checked through and was taken to the plane, it was unloaded at the front of the plane on the ground. When passengers boarded they would go to their luggage and identify each piece. Only then would it be placed on board the plane. All luggage left unclaimed would be taken back to the terminal and placed in a holding room. After identifying the luggage, the passenger could board the plane; but when we reached the top before entering, we would once again be screened with the familiar wand.

Early in the year 1992, we arranged to fly from Bombay to Saudi Arabia to visit our son who was working there at the time. A group of Indian men were on board when we flew into Riyadh. They were seeking work in Saudi and were not familiar with flying on a plane. It was a new experience for these workers.

The pilot announced that we would be landing within the hour and reminded everyone to have their cards filled out for immigration. Most of these workers (around fifty men) did not have their forms filled out. The men seated near by requested our help. They kept bringing me cards and the information to fill out their friend's card, none of which was easy to read. We filled out at least twenty cards.

The flight crew prepared for landing. Every one of these workers jumped up from their seats and started opening the overhead storage bins. They would not sit down. We tried to assist the crew, urging the men to sit down in their seats. The pilot told them to sit down, but only a few did. They actually stood with their hand luggage bracing themselves in the aisle when the plane landed. Once the plane touched down they all yelled and applauded. Ray and I looked at each other and said, "And we thought we had seen everything!" The flight crew along with the other passengers breathed a sigh of relief that nothing happened on landing that day.

A few times we would ride on a local bus. The buses were so crowded that people would be on the top of the bus and hanging on the back of the bus. A regular seat could accommodate at least three people, but they could squeeze in at least six. Then they would stand up in the aisle. It would be difficult to breathe due to the crowded conditions. We always managed to get where we were going, even if it was uncomfortable at times.

Other than the planes, we were in cars more than any other form of transportation. We were familiar with the black and yellow taxi cabs that jostled for position on the crowded streets. We learned to get a person to write out in the local language the street address we wanted so the driver would know exactly where we wanted to go. This helped on several occasions. We had established relationships with some of the drivers and they would arrange transportation for us. It was helpful to have the same person to assist us in various places.

On one occasion, we had a driver that would stop the taxi and not move forward if a cat crossed the road. He would back up a few feet and wait before moving forward. He was very superstitious, and that was his method of handling it. When it started to rain, the windshield wipers did not work. This same driver proceeded to open the window and reach with his left hand and move the wipers back and forth over the windshield. Of course, we were getting soaked in the backseat of the car; and when we told him we were getting wet from the window being down, he seemed so surprised! Just another event in the life of an itinerant missionary, trying to get to his or her place of ministry!

Chandigarh

Chandigarh is the capital of both the Punjab and the neighboring state of Haryana. The city is late-20th-century, designed by the French architect, Le Corbusier, in the 1960's. Unlike other cities in India, this city is mapped out in city blocks and has wide streets. It was the first thing I noticed upon my first visit there. The city has created a number of tourist spots around lakes and parks that add to the charm, including a large rose garden that is worth the time to visit.

Our purpose, of course, was to meet the people and to teach in a seminar which was held at the Chandigarh Baptist Church. We made a visit once a year to this church to teach, an assignment to which we looked forward. The weather was cooler in this region, our place to stay was comfortable, and the food was the best in all of India. The method of cooking curry and the seasoning they used was appealing to our palates. The men and women who gathered together from all across that region for the seminar came with their stories, testimonies, and enthusiasm for God's Word. Each place brought men and women together who had suffered for the Lord. Rejections of various forms was a part of their normal routine. It was noticeable that they were not depressed or fearful but exuded great joy in the Lord. Many of them had learned lessons that a large majority of believers never learn, "Count it all joy to suffer for Christ." James 1:2

Our host was Pastor Nazir Masih and his wife, Sarojini. Pastor Nazir was tall and very handsome. Ray mentioned to our team that Pastor Nazir was the Indian version of the

198

movie star, Cary Grant. It was evident that he and his wife were completely devoted to the work of the Lord.

Pastor Nazir was in an accident that nearly took his life in the middle seventies. He had served in ministry with Every Home Crusade but knew the Lord had other plans for him which he had ignored. He promised the Lord that he would serve Him as a pastor if he would heal him. He did recover and is still faithful serving the Chandigarh Baptist Church, which he founded in 1976.

Ten years later, he started a school out of the church for both boys and girls who could not afford an education. The school has grown rapidly with classes starting from pre nursery up through 12-plus-2, their standard. He tried for years to get the local government to surrender the land next to his church so the school could be enlarged. He felt that since he was serving the children of the community that the local officials would be sympathetic toward his need for the land. Instead they would come up with excuse after excuse. The members along with the pastor would prayer walk over the property. They erected a cement cross on the property, claiming the land in Christ's name. Whenever our team would come to teach, he would take one of the men with him to show support for the need of the property. Many hundreds were praying for that property.

Over the years, he had saved the donations that had come from various sources but did not have enough to purchase a plot of land large enough for the school. He learned that a section of land was available on the street behind the church about two or three blocks from the church. When Pastor Nazir asked how much would be required for a down payment, and when they responded, he knew that he had enough saved for the down payment. He shared, "You should have seen their expressions when I was able to give them a check for the down payment!" God had provided, and he was able to secure this piece of property for the school. His savings over the period of many years paid off with a perfect location and a large section of land for the school.

They laid the foundation in January, 1999. The building has been completed. They are now requesting another plot just behind the school so they can go to the college level. His purpose was to have a school, not only for the small children, but also one for high school age and college level. Most of all, he wanted the children to hear and learn about Christ.

The plot of land located next to the church still has not been turned over to the church, but nothing has been built on it. The church enjoys using it for outside activities.

During one of our visits to Pastor Nazir's church, Ray was teaching the book of Philippians. He experienced a startling response from the group when he read and commented on the portion, "At the name of Jesus every knee will bow, in heaven and on earth and under the earth, and every tongue confess that Jesus Christ is Lord" (Phil.2:10-11). The men stood to their feet and applauded with great gusto.

One of the men said, "All those who have rejected our message will one day bow down and admit that Jesus is Christ the Lord, the Savior of all mankind. They will know then that we told the truth!" They were filled with praise as they rejoiced together over their new insight into God's Word.

When we recall this ministry, it always brings smiles. The pastor had one of those Indian made cars that we often would call a "cartoon" car with a bubble-like, dome top. Pastor Nazir was very proud of his car and took good care of it. He had a jerky style in driving the car. He pressed the accelerator and then released it. This gave the passengers a jerk forward, and then a jerk backwards, rocking-style ride. We were always happy when the distance we traveled with him was short.

Pastor Nazir and Sarojini were perfect hosts, and we would hate to see our time come to a close. It was marvelous to see how God was using this pastor and people to bring many into His kingdom. We rejoiced that God had allowed us to know them.

Hyderabad

The capital of Andhra Pradesh is the medieval city of Hyderabad. One of their outstanding landmarks is the 16th century Charminar Gate. Early Indian rulers established themselves in Golconda, which played a very important role in Indian politics. They built a magnificent fort a few kilometres outside the city of Hyderabad. There is still a considerable Muslim presence in this city today.

In this great city, we had the privilege of working with Pastor G. Samuel. This is a man with a passion and a mission for the Lord. He was around five feet six inches and was a hard worker. Pastor Samuel started the Hyderabad Baptist Church with only twenty-five people. This pastor prayed, sacrificed, and worked hard, winning the Indian people to Christ.

Today, they have one of the largest Baptist Churches in India. On special events they can easily draw in for worship up to eight thousand in a service. On a regular Sunday attendance, they reach over five to six thousand. This church has a school, a home for orphans, medical clinic, school of evangelism, a prayer tower with members praying 24/7. The pastor and his wife live in very simple quarters on the property of the church. His children are presently grown and live elsewhere, but for many years they lived inside the church building. His entire emphasis has been placed on the church building and other buildings for the ministries. He has chosen to live on the church grounds, making him available to members at all times.

Our team was involved in teaching seminars in their school of evangelism. The last time that we taught in this ministry, there were over forty attending their school of evangelism. They had established fifty-seven chapels from their church. Today, the number has increased.

Pastor Samuel invited me to sit on the platform one Sunday morning to offer a prayer in the service. Ray was invited to preach. I could see from the platform the people coming in from the street into the grounds of the church. One woman caught my attention as she made her way down the aisle of the church to the communion table. She was dressed in a bright, pink sari and her white teeth stood out from her glowing black skin. She was smiling as she put on the table two little brown hen eggs.

Oftentimes believers would bring something they had to offer for an offering. Those people who might need the item they brought would take the item and put in an offering of rupees in the offering plate. This way everyone could give something.

I made my way to her after the service. She understood a little English but could not speak English. She spoke Tamil and Telagu. One of the young ladies in the evangelism school was my translator.

"Tell me, where are you from?" I inquired.

She proceeded to tell me that she lived in a village about three hours away from Hyderabad. She was a new believer, and she came with twelve other people to worship in the church that day. They had walked for one day to the nearest place they could get transportation. They waited for several hours before a truck came by, and they rode on the back of that truck. It took several hours to reach the city.

"I noticed you placed on the communion table two eggs. Tell me how did you bring them such a long distance?" I asked.

She was smiling broadly when she shared, "I had no money to give. My hen laid two eggs, and I carefully carried them so I could give an offering to Jesus!"

There are times when we know that the Lord is smiling; I knew this was one of those times.

Secunderbad

Secunderbad is the twin city to Hyderabad. The Centennary Baptist Church was established in 1875, many years before the Hyderabad Baptist Church. It had a long history and was the second largest Baptist Church in the area. Pastor Nala Thomas invited us to his church to recommission the men and women from his church who served all over India as missionaries. After Ray presented the sermon, the thirty-nine missionaries stood across the front of the sanctuary. A wool shawl was placed on the shoulders of each servant and a red rose given to each one of the women, along with the shawl. Ray was requested to place the shawls around each missionary, and I presented the roses to the women. Then Ray was requested to place a shawl around the pastor and his wife to rededicate them to the service of the Lord. Thinking the service was completed, we were surprised when the pastor placed a shawl around both of us. The placing of the shawl is the highest honor one can bestow on another in India. With the warmth of the shawl, I could feel the warmth of His love and protection. It was a very moving and powerful service.

Once the service was over, the associate pastor, Ephraim, requested that we go with him to see where he served. Pastor Ephraim was serving a group of new believers who were converted Muslims. They were occupying a parcel of land located under an underpass. No one wanted this land, as it was filled with rocks, and it was a place where people dumped garbage. We noticed immediately the stench on arrival. From hut to hut, we moved to speak to the

205

people and pray over each family. It was very hot outside and even more so inside the huts. Typically a hammock was strung from one side to the other. A small baby or a child was lying in the hammock. We ended up at the church building they had erected out of bamboo. It had dirt floors and no pews or chairs. We prayed for their ministry and then left. We were anxious to leave as we could not adjust to the odor. No words can describe the smell!

As we were leaving, Pastor Ephraim, who has a smile that goes all the way to his ears, tugged at Ray's arm and said something that we will never ever forget. "Pastor Rogers, God has privileged me to serve these people!"

Needless to say, we were convicted by this pastor's statement. We were anxious to leave, while he was grateful to the Lord for the privilege of serving among those people.

A year later, we returned for a seminar, and Pastor Ephraim asked us to return with him to visit his people. We braced ourselves for the experience, trying to remember our lesson from the year before. When we arrived, we could not believe the transformation that had taken place. Every thing was cleaned up. The grounds were clean, all garbage was cleared away, the huts, the little white washed bamboo church building were all cleaned, and plants were planted around the buildings.

Pastor Ephraim said to us, "When Christ comes in, He not only cleans up the inside but the outside as well."

The people were living a new life in Christ. The veil of darkness was lifted, and they began to live out their new life in Him. They understood who they were in Christ Jesus. Their actions all testified to God's goodness and mercy in their lives. The overflow was witnessing and bringing people into their church on a weekly basis. Only in Christ could this happen. In I Corinthains 2:9 it is written, "What no eye has seen nor ear heard, nor the heart of man conceived what God has prepared for those who love him." They were learning how to love and rejoice in the Lord! They had a hope and a purpose for the first time in their lives.

Khond Hills of Orissa

Each time we went to India, we would have an assignment in Orissa. Orissa was considered to be the most impoverished state of India. An agriculture project was established among the Kui tribal group in the hills of Malikapuri. An agricultural missionary was able to get a visa through an agricultural university by setting up training centers in the remote Khond Hills of Orissa. This program was highly successful and appreciated by the local people as well as the government. Some locally trained evangelist followed up on the agricultural training in the villages. As the farming methods were taught along with Bible stories, they found that they could not train people fast enough. The farmers would learn about farming by day and would hear the message of Good News by night. They prayed for the villagers. God began a mighty work in their midst.

The itinerant team was invited to be involved in the teaching aspect of this ministry. I will never forget our first journey to this remote area. We went many times throughout our seven years and always came away thanking God that we could witness this movement toward Christ.

We traveled to Bhubaneshwar and were greeted by Dr. Patra who was connected to the agricultural university located in Bhubaneshwar. He took us to his house where we were served an Indian meal made with fresh ingredients of home grown vegetables and herbs. We were given a place to rest for a short time before we began our journey into the hills. Dr. Patra took us to see several of the projects that had been started in the local area, and then we proceeded on our journey.

Upon our arrival after a five hour journey, we were taken to a house located in the yard of the Baptist Church in Malikapuri. The block house was built with funds from Dr. Owen Cooper, a Baptist layman from Mississippi. Dr. Cooper was the president of the SBC at one time.

It was a very simple dwelling with no running water. We were grateful for the well outside. A toilet, built into the floor with no seat, wasn't new to us. We were grateful to have a place with some privacy, even though the children would come in the afternoon and push the curtains aside and peer in the windows. We served as their entertainment. Three courses were taught each day, and they would gather for worship and prayer in the evenings. The meetings on some occasions were held in the church nearby the house. Other times they were held at the agricultural center.

This was a very dry area. The soil was poor, and the people of this area had very little food during the dry season. The agricultural program taught them gardening techniques and types of seeds that would grow in that soil so they could have food for their families during the long dry season.

A daily fifteen minute radio program was developed in the Kui language. This was the very first time ever to have a radio program broadcast in the Kui language. News spread as to the time the broadcast was held. Listener groups were established, and a transistor radio was given to each listener group. We were in a group on one occasion when the program was broadcast. About twenty people gathered, and they were very quiet when the program came on. The program featured health tips and agricultural information and ended by sharing the gospel. After the program was over, they talked together about what they had heard. Many came to the Lord as a result of this fifteen minute program. After the radio program began, a year later there were over five thousand Kui believers who had been baptized. The local evangelists could not keep up with the new churches started as a result of the training and the radio program. Our team went to this area twice a year, and we would stay two weeks at times.

An Unexpected Mishap in Karachi
October, 1994

The first week of October, 1994, Ray and I arrived in Karachi, Pakistan for three weeks of teaching and training. Our friends, Fred and Linda Beck, were with us for our three weeks. Three seminars were scheduled for us during the stay. Ray and I were guests of Danny and Althea Napier and their three boys. Plans were for a weekend stay in Karachi before flying on to Islamabad for the first seminar.

On Sunday evening as we were preparing for our departure the next morning, Ray said to our host, "Please don't get up to see us off in the morning. We will quietly slip out!"

"Okay!" responded Danny.

We said goodnight to everyone.

The next morning our taxi arrived to take us to the airport. Ray quietly called out, "Joyce the taxi is here!"

He had already gone to the taxi that was waiting in the driveway. As I was leaving, Danny appeared in the doorway to see us off. I moved out on the stoop of the steps to allow him room to come out of the door, saying, "You shouldn't be up!" The next thing I knew I was flying through the air. I hit my back on the crease of the steps and my head on something else. My right leg went underneath my left leg, and I knew something wasn't right.

Danny and Ray rushed to my side. "Are you okay?" they both questioned me.

"I don't know yet!" I answered, "Just let me lie here a moment!"

211

Danny rushed into the house. "I'll get some ice and some Tylenol." He came back out almost immediately with an ace bandage, some ice, a glass of water, and the Tylenol. How he did that so quickly was amazing!

Ray encouraged me to try to get up. They were able to get me to the taxi. We thought I had just taken a hard tumble and would be okay.

On the way to the airport, my right foot began to swell. Ray held my foot in his lap and applied the ice.

The Becks were staying with another family, and they arrived at the airport the same time we did. When they saw me, they exclaimed, "What happened?"

"I tried some early morning acrobats!" I said, explaining what had happened.

Between the three of them, they managed to secure a wheelchair. At our gate, Linda helped Ray wrap my foot with the bandage.

"Your foot is swelling real fast! It may be broken," mentioned Linda, worried.

I was able to use the wheelchair to the foot of the plane stairs but had to walk up the steps, a slow and painful process.

As I entered the plane, the stewardess asked, "What has happened to you?"

She immediately moved people around so I could have a seat near the door. After we were seated, Ray went to the individuals and thanked them for giving us their seats.

We were met in Islamabad by the local pastor and leader. Upon seeing me, he said, "We will get you to the hospital." We arrived at his home where tea and biscuits were served. He and Ray took me to the Women's hospital in the city. I walked in the hospital and was in a great deal of pain.

I questioned the person making the x-rays. "Do you think my foot is broken?"

He replied, "Of course, it is broken! Can't you see the bone protruding?" as he pointed to a place on the side of the foot.

I knew that it probably was broken but was holding out for good news. My immediate thoughts were, "How am I going to handle my teaching responsibilities with a broken foot?" I prayed silently, "Lord, here is something else I need for you to handle for me!"

The x-ray showed that the bone on the outside was broken, and the good news was that it was a clean break.

The next step was to see the surgeon. He examined the x-rays and the foot. "The best thing to do at this point is to wrap it well, stay off the foot until the swelling goes down, and use crutches," he advised.

I shared with him all the traveling I would be doing. "Don't you think it would be best to put it in a cast since I will be moving around a lot?"

"No, you have a clean break, and it will heal well if you stay off it until the swelling goes down. Keep it wrapped and little by little begin to use your foot!" he continued.

That afternoon, we had a two to three hour trip to the place where we would conduct our seminar. Pastors, lay-men, and some women would be arriving to study for one week. We all piled in the vehicle, and everyone made allowances for me to prop up my foot. When we arrived at the retreat grounds, we were told that we and the Becks would be staying in the apartment on the top level of a three-story building.

The Becks and Ray looked up at the building, and I looked out of the vehicle.

"How will we get Joyce to the top of that building?" they all wondered aloud. This became a serious discussion among the pastors, laymen, and us.

One suggested, "We will drive the vehicle up as close as possible to the building, and then she can crawl up the steps one by one!"

They proceeded to do so, but it had rained a lot and the steep road was slick and muddy. The car couldn't get close enough to the building. Another plan had to be devised. Finally, one of the pastors suggested that they take a straight chair and have two men on each side lift the chair up by the four legs all the way to the top.

"Mrs. Rogers, you sit in this chair!" I could see myself spilling over on those steps, but they managed to succeed in getting me to the top.

Once we got to the apartment, one of the men said, "Your students will come to you!" They had no intention of hauling me up and down those steps to the meeting hall each day!

I stayed propped up in bed or in a chair without having to move very far each day. At the appointed hour, my class would come to me. It was warm and cozy in the sitting room, and they sat on the carpet on the floor. I sat down to teach, and the informal setting caused the students to talk and share more freely. One of the students was designated to bring me my meals on a tray from the dining hall each day. They would check on me and visit with me during the week. The swelling began to go down by the end of the week.

We returned to Islamabad at the end of the week. Through the help of a friend we were able to secure a set of crutches. I had to learn how to get that certain swinging motion to move along.

As we were leaving Islamabad on Pakistani Air, the airport personnel made arrangements for me to ride the cargo elevator up to the top. They could not have been more helpful. "You can sit in the seat next to the door," the assistant said.

Once we were in Karachi, the Napiers once again opened their home to us. Each afternoon, a driver picked me up and took me to the church to teach my two hours. During the three weeks we were in Pakistan, I was able to meet all my teaching responsibilities. I have often thought about how the Lord provided for me each step of the way during this mishap. I was glad that it didn't become a stumbling block for the ministry. God showed once again how tender and gracious he is to provide all that I needed. Ray was a wonderful attentive helpmate during this mishap, and so were my missionary friends.

Ministry among the Iban People Sarawak, Malaysia

An assignment to the Iban Tribal People in Sarawak, Malaysia, took us to the longhouses in East Malaysia. We worked with a team of young people who had a ministry among the Ibans.

Eight of us in the group got in a Landrover and rode about forty-five minutes from the town of Sri Aman. The vehicle was parked at the edge of a clearing. Each one, carrying a backpack and a bottle of water, began the trek into the forest that led to the longhouse.

Our leader, Johnny, led the way on a path that had been well-trodden by folks coming and going. On occasions, the path would disappear and we found our selves walking where there was no path. They all seemed to be confident that they knew where they were going, and we gladly followed. It was an effort to keep up with them, but with determination a lot can be accomplished.

At one point, one of the young men offered to carry my backpack. He saw I was struggling, and I was grateful that he observed that I really did need some help. The path was uphill mostly, and we walked for almost an hour.

There in the middle of nowhere was a longhouse. It was nestled in at the foot of a mountain with the mountain wall directly behind the longhouse. Cocoa trees were planted all around, and beautiful pepper plant vines were every where.

In order to get up on to the veranda, we had to walk up a leaning pole cut from a coconut tree. They had hewn out places to place their feet while climbing. I watched as others made their way up the pole on to the porch without any effort before I decided to try it. I often think how funny it must have looked to all of them. They insisted on standing on each side of me until I got beyond their help, climbing higher, leaving out of their reach. I waddled my way up without falling and breaking my neck. It amazed me how Ray could get up and down these things so quickly!

Once you learned where to place your feet and how to move, it became easy. Once we were on the porch, we were escorted to the chief of the longhouse. He was a very friendly, gracious person, offering us hot tea and a cracker similar to a saltine but larger. We chatted with him, and he gave a welcome to all in the group. Once we received the welcome, we could feel free to move about the longhouse. We were informed as to where we would stay. Ray and I were given a place to stay inside the chief's quarters where we would sleep on a mattress on his living room floor.

The group shared that his wife has been ill after losing their son in a truck accident. When she heard the news of his death, she was not able to speak or to walk. She had gradually gotten worse. The chief was very anxious about her, as it had affected the entire long house.

A longhouse has anywhere from fifty families to one hundred families living under one long roof. Off the porch is a long hallway, and behind it are doors that lead to the families dwellings of those who live there. The number of doors tells how many families are represented under one roof. This longhouse had sixty doors, representing sixty families.

After the evening meal, which was all brought out and laid on mats in the long wide hallway, we had worship. They enjoyed singing for almost forty minutes. They particularly loved the choruses that were easy to memorize. After singing, we had a time of prayer. During the prayer session, they brought out the chief's wife to listen to the prayers and the message.

The team requested Ray and me to pray for her. After Ray's prayer for healing with everyone on the team placing their hands on her, they asked me to pray.

At that moment the Lord said to me, "Ask her if she wants to be well."

Looking directly into her eyes, I asked her if she wanted to be well.

She started to cry and she said, "Yes!"

I prayed, and they carried her back to her quarters.

After the service, we said *"Selamat Malam"* (good night) to all. We were fortunate that they provided a mosquito net for us. There were some flying roaches that tried to dive into the net during the night but failed to get through.

The next morning, we were surprised to see the chief's wife sitting in a chair in the kitchen. She was talking to the team members preparing breakfast. She smiled and said that she felt stronger. She attended the Bible study and the worship hour, sitting up the entire time.

After we had lunch, we packed up, said good-bye, and headed back to our vehicle. It was Saturday afternoon. Many of them would be coming into the nearby town for worship at the local church on Sunday morning.

Ray and I requested permission to leave from the chief and his wife. We prayed that the Lord would continue to strengthen her. They were so excited that she was speaking again and was able to sit up on her own.

The next morning as we prepared for worship at the church, several longhouse churches were coming together for this worship hour. They started arriving; the church filled up quickly.

A very tall Iban man arrived for worship. He was over six feet tall and very dark for an Iban. He had lots of personality and could speak English fairly well. He greeted Ray with a big hug and almost lifted him from the floor. We were told that he was the leader of the longhouse that we would visit that coming week. His name was Pak Jana.

Coming through the door were members of the group that we had visited the past few days. Who should be in the group but the chief and his wife! She actually walked and did not have to be carried. She came into the building, and everyone was excited to witness what the Lord had done in her life.

It was a powerful worship hour. The Holy Spirit was present with great power. Many were saved and healed in that worship hour.

Since that time, we have inquired about this dear woman. We were told that she became a faithful leader, giving her testimony and sharing the good news wherever she went. The last word we had from them was four years ago, and she was still faithful in her service. Just another reason to rejoice!

Pak Jana's Longhouse

Preparations were made to travel to Pak Jana's longhouse on Monday afternoon. We traveled on a major road in Sarawak, and then we cut off into a palm oil plantation traveling through the palm oil trees for about thirty minutes. We were on a dirt road that was not very safe due to rains that had left the road almost impassible. At times, the road would completely disappear, and we would be hanging in mid-air over an embankment. Several times we had to get out and walk, with only the driver taking the car through. After almost two hours, we finally reached the longhouse.

We parked the vehicle at a nearby stream. Just across the stream was a new building. The folks greeted us and took us inside their newly framed church building. It was absolutely beautiful.

Just on the other side was the worse looking longhouse we had ever seen. It looked as if you could take one finger and push it completely over. Chickens, dogs, cats, and pigs were everywhere.

We were led directly to the Chief to meet him where we were welcomed and given the traditional glass of hot tea and the saltine-type cracker.

Pak Jana asked both Ray and me to share our testimonies. They all talked about how we had Christian parents and went to church at an early age ... a privilege they did not have.

Pak Jana told us that he was formerly the witchdoctor for this longhouse, but now he was their Christian leader. He shared with us how he came to know Christ.

Then he took us outside where they had pipes coming up out of the ground that were capped with a spigot. He pointed toward a waterfall that we could see in the distance on the side of the nearby mountain. Every day, for many, many years, their people, mostly women, would make a trip to that waterfall to get buckets of water that they would carry back for their needs that day. It was a long trip that they made each day.

Pak Jana shared that when they became Christians their thought process became enlightened. They were more creative and had more insight than previously. They were inspired to pipe the water from the waterfall. He gave full credit to the leadership of the Holy Spirit who granted them the wisdom and provided additional assistance from others. He turned the water on, and it came forth with great force, almost geyser-like power. Now, they had all the water they needed, and it was pure and fresh from the mountain side.

He shared that God had told them that since they were His children that they should live like His children. They should have a nice place to gather to worship Him, and they should have a nice, clean place to live.

"It is appropriate for us to have a church first!" he added. When the church was completed, they would build a new longhouse and tear down the old one that represented their old life.

He looked directly at me and Ray and said, "Satan wanted to kill me and said that he would if I followed Jesus." He added, "I told him that he had no power over me and even if he did kill me I would always be safe in Jesus."

As we were ready to say goodnight and go to sleep, Pak Jana told me that I was the very first white woman ever to sleep in their longhouse. He questioned, "Are you afraid?"

I responded that I felt completely safe in the midst of so many believers in Christ.

He added, "It is good that the first white woman to sleep here is a Christian."

God is good!

To the Karen Refugees on the Thai-Burma Border

"I will rejoice in the Lord, I will be joyful in God my Savior"
Habakkuk 3:18

"The Lord your God is with you, he is mighty to save. He will take great delight in you, he will quiet you with His love, he will rejoice over you with singing."
Zephaniah 3:17

Leaving India after a four month teaching ministry, we were asked to go to the Karen refugees on the Thai-Burma border. We flew to Bangkok where our friend, Jim McAtee, was waiting for us. Jim had arrived from Singapore to join us in this teaching ministry on the border. This was a first-time experience for us and Jim's second visit.

A car was loaned to us by the Baptist Mission to drive to the border. Ray and I were grateful that Jim did the driving on those crowded and busy roads. The trip took around four hours to reach the small town of Mae Sot, the closest town to the border.

There are around 155,000 refugees on the border of Thailand. This refugee situation is the longest running in the world. Most of the refugees are Karens from Burma.

In 1988, Aung San Suu Kyi won 82% of the parliamentary seats as leader of the National League for Democracy (NLD). She is the daughter of one of Burma's beloved generals. Educated in England and America, she came back to Yangon to establish the National League for

223

Democracy. The opposition party, the State Law and Order Restoration Council (SLORC), refused to recognize the election results and would not hand over power to NLD. The newly elected leader, Aung San Suu Kyi, was placed under house arrest without charge or trial. The actions of the military toward Kyi's supporters were brutal, causing thousands to flee. Many who did not make it to the border were arrested or killed by the police and army. The military then changed the name of the country to Myanmar in 1989.

Huge numbers of refugees spilled out of Burma through the border of Thailand, and these refugees have been divided into groups of 10,000 or more and resituated in camps. One camp has as many as 50,000 refugees.

A pastor, who had been involved in theological education in Burma, and his wife were in one of the camps. One night when he couldn't sleep, he lay awake and talked with the Lord.

The Lord told him, "Begin a Bible School!"

He thought, "How could this be possible?!?" He began to name all the things that they didn't have, "no building, no books, no equipment or supplies... how can this be possible?"

For several days he pondered the strange thought of a Bible School in the middle of the jungle. He finally shared with his wife. Together they began to believe that it might become a reality. They prayed and asked others to join them in prayer that they would know more clearly God's direction for them.

They sensed that God did not want them to just sit and wait but to serve Him as they waited. This group that had been praying decided to take action. They put out the news

by word of mouth to the other camps announcing the pro-
posal to begin a Bible School. If anyone was interested in
preparing themselves for ministry, they were requested to
attend the meeting which was held in this pastor's camp.

Ninety-two individuals came to the meeting. They represented people from all walks of life. Some had only a high
school education, others had not finished high school, some
had university degrees, and a few had graduate degrees.
They talked about what was needed to be done in order to
begin their school. They cleared an area in the camp near
the pastor's hut for their school. The pastor sent a letter out
by a messenger to be given to someone in our Baptist
Mission in Bangkok. The letter requested materials and help
from the missionaries to teach. This is where our team came
in the picture.

We had received through our mission office in
Bangkok some information concerning our preparation for
this ministry. One suggestion was that we would need rubber boots to cross the river to get to their location. We knew
that there were no stores, no electricity, no plumbing, and
that water was brought to the camp from the river.

Jim, Ray, and I found a place to stay in Mae Sot. We
immediately set out to purchase some supplies and find our
boots. We bought some coffee, tea, rice, noodles, red beans,
cooking oil, salt and pepper, soap, etc., to take to our host,
the pastor and his wife.

After our dinner, we prayed together about what lay
ahead of us the next day. We prayed for our Father's protection and for His wisdom for the task ahead. We prayed
He might keep us well so we could serve His people.

Early the next morning, we set out to the border. It was over one hour or more by car. The countryside was peaceful, the fields rich and lush; only a few people here and there. We came upon several large elephants led by four or five men taking them to a work site to move logs. A few kilometers further we approached the Thai military check point, and they allowed us to pass through. We had been told where we could park our vehicle by the river which wasn't far from the check point.

The three of us were not too talkative as we gathered our supplies, materials for teaching, etc., and put on our boots to make our way to the refugee camp. We headed toward the river, wondering how we would manage everything and be able to get across in the water. As we neared the banks of the river, we could see a group of young people coming down the hillside across the river. They waved, and we knew they were coming to greet us. We waited for them to come across. Our young brothers in Christ Jesus greeted us with warmth and love. They took our loads and helped us across the river. I knew in my heart that all was well. Our faithful and loving Father had provided exactly what we needed. We walked back into the jungle on a well-trodden path about forty-five minutes to the pastor's bamboo bungalow.

The pastor was in his middle forties, was six feet tall, and very thin. His skin color was a caramel color. As he greeted us, tears were forming in his eyes and falling softly on his cheeks. He kept saying that he could not believe that we had come. We quickly became aware that we were speaking to a well educated man who was committed to Christ.

His wife joined us in the yard. She greeted us joyfully. She was thin and tall also. Her hair had jet-black, soft curls, which she wore shoulder length. Her face was perfectly shaped, as if sculptured. Her dark eyes sparkled as she spoke. She, too, had tears in her eyes. The pastor suggested that we join hands together and pray for the week of ministry in the Bible School and that we pray for God's protection over us. The Burmese army would often cross over on Thai soil to attack these people in their camps.

The pastor said, "I pray that it will be a quiet week, but if anything should happen, we will do all we can to protect you!"

We knew he meant every word, but we also knew that we would all have to depend on the Lord.

We were invited to place our things inside the pastor's bungalow and then walk over to the Bible School. They had built a rectangular-shaped hut which they squared off in four sections. A platform was built up front to serve as a stage. The teachers had decided what level the student would be in according to their education. Those that had degrees were placed in the front section on the right of the platform. The next group, which was directly behind the advanced group, could have been sophomores. Up front in the section on the left would be the juniors, and behind them, the freshmen. They had their own teachers, but when a guest came, they joined together for the lectures. The roof was layered leaves, the floor was dirt, the hut was opened from the roof about halfway down. Woven bamboo covered the meter high sides starting from the ground upward. Students sat on benches with no backs to them.

As we walked about getting acquainted with the camp, we could see little bamboo huts all over the mountain that blanketed the foothills in great numbers. The homes were framed on log stilts that propped them up a meter or two off the ground. The floors were slats where the ground was visible below. The roofs were made of thick, dry leaves, layered together and held by bamboo stems. The walls were made from bamboo stems, cut half long-ways and lined tightly together. Everything was of natural materials built from the Thai forest.

I taught the first two hours each morning. The pastor who spoke four languages was our translator. He stood beside me translating in Burmese from English. A short break came after my sessions. Then Ray taught for two hours. After his sessions, they took a rest break. I say "rest" as we never saw anyone eat anything during the middle of the day. Jim started his course around 2:00 and taught until 4:00 each afternoon. Our dear pastor stood by each of us for all those hours translating.

They received approximately one cup of rice per person per day. They seldom had anything to go with the rice. We figured out that they ate after dark, so it would not be noticed by those who didn't have anything. The leaders of the Bible School were truly pained that they couldn't offer us anything. When one of the students found a large stalk of bananas in the forest, they were so excited, as it meant they could offer something to their guests.

Toward the end of the week, the pastor's wife pulled me aside as I headed out to teach. She spoke softly, "Would you go with me to see my parents when you finish teaching?"

"Yes," I responded. "Do they live nearby?"

She said that they lived on the other side of the mountain. It would be about a thirty minute walk. When I finished teaching, she suggested I wear my rubber boots, and we prepared to walk to her parents' home.

While we walked together, she shared that both her dad and mom had been ill with malaria. Her mom was some better, but her dad was still very weak.

She said, "I have nothing to give my parents, but taking you to see them will be my gift to them." Her father was a military man and had supported Aung San Suu Kyi, causing him and his wife to flee or be killed. It was a bittersweet experience for them, being together as a family but under severe conditions. They had been on the border for three years

As we went over the crest of the hill, there were hundreds of little huts nestled down in the valley. As we approached her parents' place, I could see a gentleman leaning against the steps in front of the hut. He stood up straight as we got closer.

He was a tall man, over six feet with a large frame, but he was very thin. His shining silver hair was striking against his caramel-tan complexion. In greeting me, his blue grey eyes were clear and penetrating. He smiled and welcomed me with a strong handshake. We spoke together briefly before going inside their place.

"At first I thought we would be here two or three months, but it has been three years now," he exclaimed. He was a high ranking military officer and had had a good life in Burma. He was well educated and could speak several languages. His English was impeccable.

We went inside where his wife was seated with nine-teen beautiful kindergarten aged children. She was an older version of her daughter. Her black, naturally curly, hair and dancing sparkling eyes matched her vivacious personality. She acted as if we were old friends meeting again.

The children sang songs in English, Burmese and Thai languages. They quoted scripture verses; and then, one by one, they shook hands with me before they were dismissed to go to their homes.

She talked about preparing the children for the day they could return to their home country. It was important that they be educated so they would be prepared. Then she added, "The most important of all is that they will know Jesus as their Savior!"

Throughout the week, I had given a great deal of thought about the plight of the refugees. I thought about what they must be thinking and feeling. I couldn't imagine what it must be like not to be able to go to one's own home country. Yet, no one complained to us. Many did not know the circumstances of their own family or friends back in their home country. Some did not have official papers of identification. There were no telephones, no stores, no hospital, and only huts for homes and schools. They did not even have the freedom of going to a nearby town. They were "parked" there with little or no help from any-one at that time.

As the four of us sat together, I directed my question to the father. "Would you share with me how you process the situation you find yourself in? Do you ever feel that God has forgotten you?"

He looked at me with those blue grey eyes and said, "We don't always know why things happen as they do, but I do know that God is with us. God doesn't always remove us *from* the situation, but he comes and dwells with us *in* the situation."

He continued speaking with conviction, "My prayer is that we will one day be able to return to our beloved Burma. I pray that my wife, those kindergarten children, my dear daughter and son-in-law, all the Bible school students will be able to return." Then he added, "If I don't make it back, then my life will live on through their extending my witness for Christ."

We prayed together. I prayed for them, and they prayed for me and my family, and for Jim.

He said, "We will most likely never see you again on earth, but we will see each other in heaven!" We embraced each other with tears coming down our faces.

As the pastor's wife and I walked back to her place, she thanked me for allowing her to bless her parents through me.

I told her, "You blessed me! Thank you for allowing me to meet your parents." I was truly the one that had been blessed.

She smiled, and we walked together in silence for a while.

I thought back over what had happened during that visit. My Lord had allowed me to witness faith-in-action. I kept thinking about what the father had said, "God doesn't always remove us *from* the situation, but He comes and dwells with us *in* the situation!" Even though forsaken by their leaders in their country, they stood strong in faith because they knew God had not forsaken them.

Time arrived for us to leave. They requested that the three of us stand on the stage. They had made a lei for us out of greenery they had found in the forest around them. Someone had made a traditional vest-type garment which they presented us.

They expressed regrets that they couldn't give us something, but the pastor announced that the students would sing for us. They stood up from where they were seated and preceded to sing Handel's "Hallelujah Chorus." I looked at Ray and Jim and tears were coming down their cheeks. There we were out in the jungle on the Thai border with the blue sky above, and I knew that our Lord was looking down at that group of believers smiling because they were praising Him.

We said our good-byes, and a small group walked with us down the mountain path to our vehicle. Jim, Ray, and I agreed that we had been blessed beyond measure.

As I continued to pray for this group that we had come to know and love, Ray pointed out to me a passage in Habakkuk that could be the testimony of the father. Habakkuk did not understand why God was allowing an evil nation to rule over the people of Judah. He argued with God about it. Then he came to the place where he knew that faith in God alone would answer his questions. He was able to say with conviction the following as a testimony of God's faithfulness:

"Though the fig tree does not bud and there are no grapes on the vines, though, the olive crop fails and the fields produce no food, though there are no sheep in the pen and no cattle in the stalls, yet I will rejoice in the Lord, I will be joyful in God my Savior. The Sovereign Lord is my strength; he makes my feet like the feet of a deer, he enables me to go on the heights." (Habakkuk 3:17-19)

I recently learned that four years ago the father passed away. He didn't make it back to his beloved Burma! Even as you read this personal account, thousands are still living on the border. Some have been resettled in Australia and only recently in America. They need our prayers.

Conclusion

I am so grateful that the Lord called Ray and me to serve Him as International Missionaries. He gave to us the blessing of meeting and serving so many choice people in many different countries. The journey was not always easy, but He never failed us. He gave to us the power of the Holy Spirit to lead people out of their darkness into His light. There are still many waiting to hear the good news. Yes, there are still those who are up to their knees in mud in those rice paddy fields, not knowing that there is a God above who loves them. We praise Him that we were used to bring some of those people to a knowledge of Christ and His love for them.

This book has been in process for at least four years. Over the years, various ones have encouraged us, "Write your story." When we spoke in churches, some would suggest that we should write a book. Time and time again we would hear those words, "You should write a book!"

I felt that it was beyond reach until the Holy Spirit started nudging me. I fought the idea. I kept asking, "How can this be?"

I do my best praying and thinking when I wake in the middle of the night. It was one of those nights when the Lord placed in my heart the desire to begin writing our mission story. I knew that He wanted the story told.

I am well aware that this book only represents a portion of the stories and experiences of our thirty-five year missionary journey. Some things could not be shared due to the time in which we live. I intentionally did not give the names of some individuals due to their situations.

Since our retirement in June 1998, we have been blessed by returning to Malaysia, serving in Karachi, Pakistan; Myanmar (Burma); and Banda Aceh, Indonesia. We also visited Hanoi in 2002. Each of these ministries bring to our minds and hearts the faces and memories of people who touched us, and for whom we pray we touched as well.

As you come to the conclusion of this book, I ask you, have you accepted Christ as your Lord and Savior? I invite you to open your heart and receive Him as Lord and Savior of your life. This is the most important decision you will ever make! You may pray a prayer similar to this as you call on God to save you:

"Lord Jesus, I am a sinner. I repent of my sin. I believe you died for me on the cross and rose again. I turn away from my sin and place my faith in Jesus Christ. I receive you in my life. Thank you for saving me. In Jesus' name I pray, Amen."

Once you have received Jesus into your life, please tell a pastor or another Christian about your decision. Go to church and show others your faith by asking for baptism by immersion in your local church.

From my thirty-five years on the foreign mission field, I would encourage you that whatever you may face in life, always allow it to draw you to the Master. The heartaches and difficulties of life help to reshape you in His image and to His glory when you allow Him control over you. Learn how to be grateful, praise Him in every situation, and give thanks in everything. When you do this, it will take the sting out of the difficulty and give you joy.

As Habakkuk 3:18 says, "I will *rejoice* in the Lord, I will be joyful in God my Savior."

Photo Gallery

Joyce, age 2

**Joyce's parents, S. Mortimer and
Bessie Garrision Campbell**

Ray's parents, Jessie Clifton and Flossie Rogers cut the cake at their Fiftieth Wedding Anniversary

Ray, Joyce, John in 1967

Joyce's parents with brothers, sisters, nieces and nephews in May, 1968

Christopher John Rogers, age 5

Seventh-Day Adventist Hospital in Penang

Georgetown Baptist Church in Penang in 1963

Our freight was unloaded manually in Kediri.

Marhaen **(Communist youth marching)**

Happy

Ray baptizes believers in a village near Kediri.

Ngadiredjo Baptist Church

Ngadiredjo congregation

Lemani (left)
with brother
and sister

Joyce teaches
U.S. geography to
fifth graders,
John Rogers and
Cliff McAtee in
school in Kediri.

Barney

Joyce speaks at a women's meeting in Indonesian Kain-Kebaya in April, 1970.

**Indonesian girl who stayed in
Ray and Joyce's home**

**Graduates of 1982, with John in the middle, in front of
the American flag.**

**Some members of Pak Matadji's family,
along with Eli and his dad**

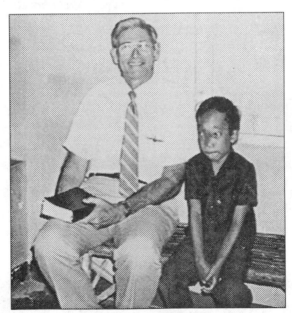

Ray sitting with Eli

Congregation of Clendon Baptist Church in New Zealand

Pastor G. Samuel and his associate in Hyderabad, India

Hyderabad Baptist Church congregation

Longhouse Evangelism team in Sarawak

Longhouse *serambi muka* (front porch)

Pastor Ephraim's congregation in Secunderabad, India

**Ray prays for the missionaries from the
Centennary Baptist Church in Secunderabad**

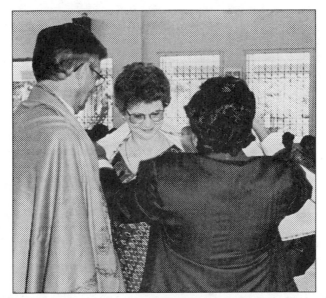

Pastor Nala Thomas places the shawl of commissioning around Joyce as Ray watches.

Ephraim, Pastor Thomas, and Ray stand in front of Ephraim's church

Ray and Joyce in
Hyderabad, India

Pastor Nazir Masih in
Chandigarh, India

Joyce in an Indian sari

Service in Orissa

Joyce and Ray in front of Taj Mahal

Seminar in Visakhapatnam, India

Ray and Joyce experience a camel ride in Karachi.

Seminar in Nepal

Ray preaches at the International Church in Karachi.

Cell group in Penang, Malaysia

Kin Choy and his family with Ray and Joyce

Our next door neighbors in Penang

Time of retirement, 1998

Ray sits with his grandsons, William Lewis (left) and Christopher Ray (right) in June, 2005.

Christopher Ray and granddad Ray in Indonesia, 2007

Works Cited

Map of India. On-line. Internet. 2 February 2008.
Available: http://worldatlas.com/webimage/countrys/asia/
outline/inout.htm

Rogers, Joyce. Personal letters and journal, plus newsletters, and reports to Indonesia Baptist Mission. 1965-1972.

Smith, Ebbie. *God's Miracles: Indonesian Church Growth*.
South Pasadena, CA: William Carey Library. 1970.